RAISING LAMBS AMONG WOLVES

RAISING LAMBS AMONG WOLVES

How to Protect Your Children from Evil

Mark I. Bubeck

MOODY PRESS

CHICAGO

ISBN: 0-8024-7194-3

5 7 9 10 8 6 4

Printed in the United States of America

To my long-time friends and esteemed spiritual leaders,
Warren and Betty Wiersbe.
Without their encouragement and helpful suggestions,
my writing ministry would not have happened.

CONTENTS

ACKNOWLEDGMENTS

My deepest appreciation goes to those numerous friends and counselees who granted me the privilege of using stories from their lives to clarify and illustrate the application of spiritual freedom. Utmost care has been exercised to protect each from being identified. In some cases, not only the names but gender and place have been changed. Similarities of experiences have even led to some accounts becoming a composite picture from two or more persons. Each illustrating account comes from the true experiences of people who graciously approved my use of their story. Such accounts make the application of biblical truth come to life. For that I am deeply thankful.

A special note of thanks is due my immediate family. My wife, Anita, each of my three daughters, and their families have contributed to this work. Some accounts from their lives are identified but others are not. I am humbled by their loving trust of me and their supportive desire to contribute to the message of this book.

INTRODUCTION

And there shall be a time of trouble,
Such as never was since there was a nation, . . .
Those who are wise shall shine
Like the brightness of the firmament,
And those who turn many to righteousness
Like the stars forever and ever.
(Daniel 12:1b, 3, NKJV)

These prophetic words from the angelic messenger to Daniel and to us have a message for our times. The troubles upon the nations of the world are mounting up like nothing that has ever been. There seem to be few voices that would dispute the mounting evidence of world chaotic trouble. Even as I pen these words, the telecast has just announced of a gunman invading a kindergarten class in a peaceful rural setting in Scotland. With four guns blazing he murdered sixteen kindergarten children and their teacher.

"Trouble . . . Such as never was . . ." These prophetic thoughts help focus the message of this book. The troubled darkness of this hour is very great. And yes, children are in danger. Not of mass murder from a crazed gunman, of course. The dangers are more subtle than that. But they are also more pervasive. Children, in their innocence, are vulnerable to the wolves in American society. Those wolves are everywhere, but their main attacks come on the home. Here parents must protect their children and prepare them for living one day on their own.

Families comprise an institution that God has made the bulwark of civilization, and families are under calamitous assault—all the forces of hell seem to be conspiring to destroy the home. Divorce has devastated many families. The homosexual lifestyle is being championed as the socially and politically correct issue of the hour; its proponents say they are "family" too, and some have even succeeded in adopting children as part of their own family units. Spiritism in all its forms is clamoring for acceptance from New Age books and entertainment. For our children, even some toys and the public school curricula have spiritistic elements.

In the midst of this increasing darkness, God has placed the Christian family. God has ordained that godly parents shine with sufficient light to turn their own children to righteousness and truth. As we shine in compassionate, protective oversight of our own children, God uses us as the light amid the darkness of the nations and the salt that dispels corruption in the world.

A vital way we parents can protect our children is through prayer, particularly what I term "doctrinal prayer." Such prayer rests upon the absolutes of truth available to believers through the finished work of our Lord Jesus Christ. Such prayer has a deeper foundation than the loving, emotional desires of a protecting parent. Doctrinal prayer enables loving parents to apply the victories won for us by our Lord Jesus Christ directly against the efforts of evil wolves seeking to capture our children. The pattern prayers appearing throughout this book (and which comprise most of the final chapter) have proven helpful in this effort. I commend them to you as a vital way to use doctrinal truth as you pray on behalf of your children.

The purpose of this book is to help Christian parents appropriate and use God's Word and doctrinal praying to provide protection for their children. Christian parents do not need to fail because of the darkness in which they live. Light dispels darkness. Wolves hunt and roam most effectively under cover of night. To chase them away—to protect our children— we must shine the light around our children.

Truth not only sets us free but enables us to parent in freedom. Turning our children from darkness to the light of righteousness makes a parent shine *"like the stars forever and ever."* My prayer is that God will use this book to help parents be shining stars.

PART ONE

HELPING OUR LAMBS: FROM ONE GENERATION TO ANOTHER

CHAPTER ONE

FOOTPRINTS IN THE CARPET

L inn came quietly into the kitchen where her mother was busily preparing the meal. A vivacious junior in college, Linn seemed pensive, as if spiritually moved. Her bouncy zip was subdued, her mood sober. Emotions were near the surface; in fact as she spoke, her eyes were brimming with tears. "Mom, is Dad still going into our rooms every night like he did before we went to college to pray for Peter and me?"

Chris was not prepared for the question. She knew Ted was dedicated to his long-standing, intercessory prayer vigils for their children, and she respected his dedication and heart. The prayers were a very private and sincere matter with her husband. Now she wondered how to respond to her daughter's question. Her daughter's directness seemed to necessitate a straightforward response.

"Yes, he is," Chris answered, "but how did you know?"

"I saw his footprints in the carpet," Linn replied. "I never knew that would mean so much to me!" The tears were coming more freely now. "I guess I'm growing up and my value system is different."

I'll relate the full story of Ted, Chris, and their children later, but Linn's response to her father's prayers should be noted here. Her tears of appreciation show us how parents can leave "footprints" in their children's lives, footprints children often follow. Footprints that can lead them away from wolves and along a path of safety. Sadly, we must recognize that children often follow a different path, guided by a more uneven set of footprints.

WOUNDS FROM OUR PARENTS

Physical, Sexual, or Verbal Abuse

"Oh Mommy, Mommy, please let's not go home yet!" The little girl, perhaps three or four, was pleading for help. "Please, please, Mommy! Don't make me go home yet. Daddy will yell at me and yell at me. Oh please, Mommy, please, don't make me go home. Please, Mommy, please!"

My wife overheard these words spoken by the frantic little child while shopping in our town. "My heart was almost torn out by her frantic, pitiful pleading," my wife confessed. "I wanted to gather her in my arms, quiet her trembling body and frightened emotions, and reassure her of my love and protection."

The department store elevator stopped and the mother exited with her frantic child. My wife, Anita, continued shopping, trying to forget the encounter. But the cry of a hurting child would not leave her ears. About an hour later as my wife made her way to her parked car, she encountered the family again. The little girl was still pleading, "Oh, please, Mommy, don't make me go home! Daddy will yell at me and hurt me!"

We do not know the mother and daughter; we would never learn the whole story behind those frantic pleas that lasted for more than an hour. But the sad, dejected countenance of the mother offered strong support to the possibility that a mean-spirited husband and father awaited at home. Abusive husbands and abusive fathers are much too common in the culture of our times.

The hurts that are harvested from abusive parental actions and words go on and on. A healthy recovery is very difficult. Often years later the pain emerges from the wounded; the hurts are still near the surface. Crisis circumstances develop and the unresolved hurts come roaring into view. Often they require extensive therapy and patient counseling. As a parent, be aware that the first place the wolves may attack your children is through you. If you are a victim of abuse, for example, be alert to how you may pass destruction on to your children. And be aware that such sin can keep your children from seeing and believing in a good and gracious heavenly Father.

Anita and I recently received a loving letter from a young mother who had been a part of our pastoral ministry many years ago. Jenny reminded us of how we had been there to help during a very dark time in their family life. Dad was verbally, physically, and sexually abusive to Jenny and her sibling brothers and sisters. Jenny wrote of the recent death of her beloved brother while he was undergoing surgery.

"It was difficult and sad. He was really quite unhealthy for a long time. He had lung cancer in '88 and almost died from pneumonia. He lived a hard life—smoking, drinking, and drugs. But, I know him as a child—and I know of his childhood. He was a really good person deep inside—in his heart. I will miss him. I don't know for sure if he was a Christian or not. I am pretty sure that he received Christ as a little child. He highly respected you, Pastor. . . .

"It's hard to believe in a loving heavenly Father when your earthly father was as cruel and abusive as ours was. You are extra special, Pastor, I have always believed that you represented the Lord Jesus to us all. You were a good father image. Thanks for everything! I hope that Bob is in heaven, but I won't know for sure until I get there."

Jenny's letter spoke deeply to me. It spoke of the awful hurt and fearful destruction wrought in a child's life from parental abuse. Yet, despite her kind, commending words, Jenny's letter also humbled me and spoke to me of the need for deeper, more godly sensitivity. Bob had heard the gospel in my sermons, but I had never confronted him personally about his need to know Jesus Christ. The loving respect he later verbalized about me had provided me an open door of opportunity other pastors didn't have. Those who minister God's love to abused children have strategic opportunities to reach and heal the hurting.

The redeeming, healing power of our Lord Jesus Christ is sufficiently strong to set people free from the brutalizing, wounding consequences of even parental abuse. Jenny and several of her sisters are living testimonies of this truth. God's grace knows no abusive activity too detrimental or too destructive for it to transform and heal. Parents can recover from their own abuse to become strong lights that repel the wolves that threaten their children.

A pastor friend provides a living example of this truth. Tom was orphaned as a very young child. Though emotionally torn by the loss of his mother and father, Tom had the added misfortune of being placed in an orphanage where unfair and cruel discipline was regularly administered. Some of the dark experiences he related about that place still make me shudder to remember. Yet, those very traumas were used by God's redeeming grace and sovereign plan to mold Tom into one of the most compassionate pastors I have ever known. He also was a tremendous dad. In his role as both a father and husband, Tom was exemplary. My wife and I met Tom and his wife again at a recent conference. It was a special joy to learn that the children of this retired couple are faithfully walking with their Lord. Abusive experiences need not always bring ruin to the abused.

Other Ways Parents Can Wound Children

You may not have been the victim of abuses such as those described. Yet you may have become vulnerable to the attack of the wolves of darkness because of other harmful acts of parents not commonly labeled abuse. If you are now a parent, you have the opportunity to correct or avoid common pitfalls.

Here are a few things to watch against and correct quickly if they are practiced in your life (by yourself or by your parents):

1. Failing to commend the child for accomplishments, while implying he or she could have done a better job.

2. Making negative comments about any aspect of a child's appearance, intelligence, or worth.

3. Failing to include personal time with each child daily, letting work schedules and personal pursuits override such times.

4. Praising one child's accomplishments above another's.

5. Comparing the child negatively with someone else (including a brother or sister).

6. Breaking promises to a child that the child highly valued (for example, a fishing trip, sports event, or gift you had promised).

7. Claiming to be someone before others outside the family but not acting that way in the home. Such hypocrisy does more to negate positive influence on a child than anything else.

8. Using fear to gain a desired behavior. (For example, "If you eat that you might get sick and die"; "God will punish you if you dirty Mom's floor.")

9. Yelling at the child in frustration or impatience.

10. Never apologizing to your child even when you know you "blew it" in some matter.

THE DELAYED HARVEST

If we, as parents, practice such behaviors, we should beware, for we are leaving our lambs open to the wolves. They are vulnerable to having the negative family legacy described in both the Old and New Testament. The legacy is part of a biblical principle I call "the delayed harvest."

The Principle

The apostle Paul describes the delayed-harvest principle well in his letter to the Galatians:

> Do not be deceived, God is not mocked; for whatever a man sows, that he will also reap. For he who sows to his flesh will of the flesh reap corruption, but he who sows to the Spirit will of the Spirit reap everlasting life. (Galatians 6:7–8, NKJV)

The apostle reminds us of one of life's most basic facts: We reap what we sow. But his words also should remind us that *others also reap from the seeds we've sown.* This seed sowing may be for good or evil. Whatever we plant in the lives of our own children eventually will yield a harvest. It may be delayed, but the harvest will come. The delayed harvest, written in the lives of those we influence, is probably the most significant part of this sowing-reaping syndrome.

There is a delayed harvest, reaped in the lives of children. When we sin, the consequences are more than personal guilt and personal harm. Our sins have a longer arm of consequence. In the majestic context of God's judicious holiness, Moses learned this truth from Almighty Jehovah Himself.

> Now the Lord descended in the cloud and stood with him there, and proclaimed the name of the Lord. And the Lord passed before him and proclaimed, "The Lord, the Lord God, merciful and gracious, longsuffering, and abounding in goodness and truth, keeping mercy for thousands, forgiving iniquity and transgression and sin, by no means clearing the guilty, visiting the iniquity of the fathers upon the children and the children's children to the third and the fourth generation." So Moses made haste and bowed his head toward the earth, and worshiped. (Exodus 34:5–8, NKJV)

Its Application

Texts like this have profound and difficult implications. In a later chapter we will consider the theology of children suffering because of their parents' sins and their grandparents' sins. But God clearly articulates a principle in His declaration to Israel: a "delayed harvest" has come.

As mentioned above, this harvest may bring either harm or blessing to children. In the case of Linn, her father's prayers yielded a blessing. We can transfer blessings from one generation to another. Exodus 20:6 speaks of God "showing love to a thousand generations of those who love me and keep my commandments." Godly living also has a long arm of benefit and blessing that may be transferred from one generation to another. The apostle Paul seems to make reference to this transference of blessing when he writes to Timothy, "I have been reminded of your sincere faith, which first lived in your grandmother Lois and your mother Eunice and, I am persuaded, now lives in you also" (2 Timothy 1:5).

Such godly living does not mean our children will automatically follow God or be immune from sin's temptations. Consider Solomon, the wise king who in later years served God only halfheartedly. Solomon benefited from the transferred blessing because of the godly ways of his father, David. After Solomon had fallen into grievous sins at the close of his reign, God pronounced this judgment: "Since this is your attitude and you have not kept my covenant and my decrees, which I commanded you, I will most certainly tear the kingdom away from you and give it to one of your subordinates. Nevertheless, for the sake of David your father, I will not do it during your lifetime. I will tear it out of the hand of your son" (1 Kings 11:11–12). Solomon's choices to sin and do evil left little blessing to pass on to his generational lineage, but he was able to continue to benefit from his father's godly living.

There are wonderful generational benefits from living for our Lord Jesus Christ. Recently my brother showed me a copy of a newspaper obituary of my great-grandfather. Some of our relatives had kept it all of these years, and now I read with wonder and joy two columns of text extolling the Christian character and spiritual ministry of my great-grandfather. A lay Christian, Great-grandpa Bubeck did extensive preaching and teaching of the Word of God. I know that I, my brothers, and our families all enjoy a direct tie to that godly man in our generational lineage.

Generational blessings do transfer, as we'll see in the next chapter. For the Bubecks, God has blessed my four brothers and me with Christian families who are following Christ. God has made it the passion of my heart that the "delayed harvest" flowing from my life will pass on the same blessings I enjoy

from my great-grandfather. What wonderful promises of grace
God has given us to claim.

A Negative Harvest

As parents, we must face the fact, however, that the
"delayed harvest" may be very harmful if our lives have been
sinful and wicked. God will visit "the iniquity of the fathers
upon the children and the children's children to the third and
the fourth generation" (Exodus 34:7b, NKJV). Those are awesome, staggering words. No wonder that on hearing them
Moses immediately fell on his face there on the mountain and
worshiped the Lord. Who can fathom such far-reaching
accountability to God? Who can measure what harmful, disastrous hurt our sins may effect in the lives of those we cherish
the most?

Yes, Solomon reaped the benefit of his father David's godly
life. Yet we must also recognize that he also experienced the consequences flowing from David's most glaring sins. Solomon's
failures were centered in his giving in to sensual sins. He followed a pattern of sexual sins. His sensual love for foreign,
beautiful women was legendary. He married seven hundred
women and had three hundred additional concubines to satisfy
his perverted sexual appetites. As he grew older, these foreign
women influenced Solomon to follow their idolatrous practices. This spelled his doom. As the chronicler of 1 Kings noted:

> Solomon did evil in the eyes of the Lord; he did not follow the
> Lord completely, as David his father had done.
> The Lord became angry with Solomon because his heart
> had turned away from the Lord, the God of Israel, who had
> appeared to him twice. Although he had forbidden Solomon to
> follow other gods, Solomon did not keep the Lord's command.
> (1 Kings 11:6, 9–10)

Solomon's moral sins had a direct relationship to one of
David's darkest failures. The "delayed harvest" principle was at
work. At some point Solomon learned about his father's sin
with his mother Bathsheba and the proxy murder of Uriah.
Solomon had a direct tie to that sin as the second son of David

and Bathsheba. David's sexual sins, though not as extensive as Solomon's, are well catalogued in God's Word. The tragedy of moral failure and idol worship didn't stop with Solomon. The descendants of this brilliant, wise king fell into the "delayed harvest" of Solomon's wicked practices and the whole nation of Israel deteriorated. Eventually both Israel and Judah fell into captivity for their idolatrous ways. When there is no regeneration and transformed correction, the "delayed harvest" can go on and on until God's wrath brings fierce judgment.

Ted's footprints in the carpet give us the clue as parents on how to march through fields full of weeds and dangerous enemies and produce for our children a good harvest. As we shall see, the answers are found in warfare prayers and knowing doctrinal truths.

WOLVES AND DOCTRINAL PRAYERS

The Brandons (not their real name), a mature Christian couple, had adopted Clarissa when she was just three days old. In the Brandon home little Clarissa received lots of the tender loving care, discipline, and educational opportunity that should be a part of every child's early years. She also participated in the weekly church school and worship services at a strong evangelical church. Despite these exemplary opportunities, Clarissa became increasingly difficult to handle. Rebellion, cursing, violent actions, and bizarre behavior patterns caused her parents to seek professional help. The psychiatrist and social workers finally expressed their defeat by recommending that the Brandons consider permanently institutionalizing Clarissa.

THE POWER OF DOCTRINAL PRAYER

Clarissa's Story

At age ten, Clarissa was considered too dangerous for her parents or any other guardian to handle. Her acts of violence had increased, and attending a public or private school was not possible. Her disruptiveness and danger toward the other children were constant.

Clarissa's parents had prayed often through this ordeal. Now, in God's sovereign answer to those prayers, they were in a serious search for a spiritual answer. They read my books on biblically balanced spiritual warfare and called me for counsel. I suggested that they seek to find out all they could about her bloodline parentage. The Brandons brought Clarissa to see me for personal counseling. It was not possible to counsel directly with Clarissa. She was totally uncooperative. So the counsel time had to focus on the parents.

The Brandons told me they had learned through a friend of the biological parents about their lifestyles. Both had lived and were continuing to live very wickedly. Between the two, prostitution, witchcraft, drug usage, and severe alcoholism had become common. Listening to this recounting of Clarissa's past, I realized that generational sin might be at work.

At my suggestion, the parents began to aggressively pray on their adopted daughter's behalf. They left my office instructed to claim their rightful place in asserting protective parental authority over Clarissa in the spiritual realm. They firmly resisted the Enemy. Powers of darkness that might try to claim controlling influence over Clarissa because of the sins lived out by her biological parents were resisted through prayer. The Brandons steadfastly opposed any demonic influences. They asked the Lord Jesus Christ to sever any bloodline claims against Clarissa by the powers of darkness. If they witnessed behavior that caused them to suspect attempts by the wolves of darkness to rule and control Clarissa, they used the kind of prayer resistance advocated in the final chapter of this book.

As the Brandons claimed their spiritual positions of authority and protective oversight over Clarissa, remarkable change for the better began to come. It was so remarkable that the social workers could not believe the difference. We will look at the specifics at a later time, but the response of the Brandons should remind us that specific, doctrinally based prayers do help us overcome the wolves in our children's lives, and can even diminish or eliminate the effects of a "delayed harvest" in their lives.

Suzy's Story

Several years ago I met with a young professional couple concerned about their five-year-old daughter; we'll call them the Dengles. They sought my counsel because Suzy would regularly lose control of herself in violent rages. The problem became so severe that Mary Dengle one day called her husband at his professional office. "Jim, you must come home immediately." Mary spoke with urgency. "I'm afraid of our daughter." These were not the words of an hysterical wife. Mary was calm but very alarmed. Suzy was using what seemed like abnormal strength to overpower her mother even though she was a small five-year-old. Though Suzy had lived a sheltered life in their Christian home, cursing and vile threats accompanied her out-of-control rages. During these episodes discipline was completely ineffective.

During the first counseling session with Jim and Mary Dengle, I asked them if anyone in either side of their family lineage had shown similar, out-of-control anger rages. When problems of this nature appear in such young children, the possibility of generational "delayed harvest" needs to be considered. Jim and Mary both looked at each other and smiled. Though reared in a religious home, Jim had only become a believer during his professional training years. He revealed that his father had abused Jim during several violent, out-of-control rages. Now that Jim was a believer, he was trying to find release from bitterness and true forgiveness of his father for the many cruel beatings he had received as a child.

I discussed with the Dengles the principle of sowing and reaping and the "delayed harvest"; then I suggested a spiritual plan to help their little Suzy. The plan was simple. The next time Suzy would begin her out-of-control behavior, Jim was to

respond by gently gathering her into his arms. Confining her
flaying arms, scratching fingers, and kicking legs in his mascu-
line strength, he was to pray over her in this fashion:

*Heavenly Father, in the name of my Lord Jesus Christ and by the
power of His blood, I renounce any generational rage that is seeking to control Suzy. I forbid all such control and I ask the Holy
Spirit to calm and control Suzy by His loving presence and control
of her mind, will, emotions, and body.*

A remarkable change took place the first time Jim followed those instructions. Suzy was completely out of control.
She was so violent and strong, Jim wondered if he could hold
on to her, but he gave it a try. She screamed, cursed, and
attempted to bite him, but he began to pray quietly as suggested. As he prayed he felt her relaxing. In the midst of his prayer,
she turned her face to his, kissed him on the cheek by his ear,
and said with tender feeling, "I love you, Daddy!"

This was the beginning of a wonderful change in Suzy's
life. Her parents continue to protect her by their prayers and
teach her how to overcome her anger in a biblical way. On a
recent visit to their city, I was privileged to see a beautiful little
girl now maturing into a godly young person.

MISCONCEPTIONS ABOUT GOD
AND THE "DELAYED HARVEST"

Reading these two accounts, you may be thinking, *Such
prayer and loving parents may help in many cases, but you can't
always escape the legacy of your parents.* Besides being a pes-
simistic attitude, such thinking disregards our resources in
Christ as well as the love that God has for us and His willingness to help. Here are three common misconceptions about
reaping from our parents' sins that we must recognize.

"I Am Doomed to Failure"

1. *"I am doomed to failure because of the sinful acts of my
generational heritage."* Counselors often hear statements like

these during the counseling session:

> "My mother was nothing but a dope head and I come by my addiction to drugs in keeping with the family tradition."
>
> "Our whole family has been klutzy from day one. I was born a klutz and I'll always be a klutz."
>
> "My dad was an alcoholic and I guess I'm doomed to be one too."

Doom, defeat, despair, and constant guilt plague many because of their perceived tie to the negatives of their family heritage. But God's saving grace changes lives. Of course, I'm not implying that coming to know Christ immediately solves all problems. Salvation does not set everyone free from all the depressive harm and wounded emotions of one's hurtful past. Time, nurture, and loving counsel may be very much needed. But a personal relationship with God through His Son Jesus Christ is the starting place. Be sure of your spiritual salvation in Christ. You may need to seek counseling help. Most important, recognize that ultimate freedom rests firmly on the certainty that regeneration power and resurrection life have entered one's life.

Doom and defeat marked Jessica's life. I remember her so well. I spoke at a church conference one week in a small Minnesota town and observed Jessica during the first meeting. Seated with her husband, Fred, in the second row, she communicated pain. Gloom and despair were etched into her face. Body language shouted, "I am hopeless." I avoided looking at her when I taught because her countenance was so distracting.

The pastor encouraged those desiring counsel time with me during the conference to arrange appointments through him. After the service, the pastor informed me that several requests had come. I responded by saying, "I hope one is that lady who sits with her husband in the second row." Hers was the first request. I prayerfully looked forward to helping one with such obvious hurting needs.

When we met together, Jessica informed me that she came

from a very dysfunctional family. Her mother and father had been alcoholics and "drug heads," as she called them. She and her siblings had been victims of much abuse. Anger, bitter hurt, and the doom of failure ruled Jessica's heart. Dark despair filled every thought of her mind.

I asked Jessica to share her salvation experience with me. A works-centered hope of gaining eternal life poured out of Jessica's testimony. She did everything at the church without anyone even asking her. She was faithful to every service. I knew where we needed to start.

Jessica needed to understand God's grace. We spent the next hour looking into the Word of God about salvation. The Holy Spirit granted spiritual understanding. She invited the Lord Jesus Christ into her life to save her from all of her guilt and lostness. She asked Him to remove all the hurt, anger, and harm from her dysfunctional background. I led her in a renunciation of any claim the kingdom of darkness was holding against her because of her own sins or those of her generational lineage.

The change was dramatic. We walked out of the pastor's parsonage study. Observing her changed countenance, the pastor and his wife exclaimed, "What happened to you, Jessica?" The radiance of Christ was shining. As the Lord poured in His joy, exuberance bubbled over. Like the woman at the well in John 4, Jessica's cup was full and running over.

At the evening service, everyone noticed. People kept saying: "It's obvious something good has happened in your life." Joyfully she told of her spiritual salvation. A radiant peace leaped out with a compelling message. The darkness was gone. In its place was peace and light. There is a beauty to healed forgiveness that the Lord sometimes lets us see in people like Jessica.

There is more beauty to Jessica's story, but the message for this moment is clear. The saving grace of Christ is sufficient to free all who come to Him. The hurts and harms of our dysfunctional past fall in defeat before God's saving grace.

Jessica's story reminds us that people sometimes go through profession of faith, baptism, church membership and all the motions of church life without experiencing the new birth. The darkness of Jessica's past was still there. Cleansing and healing grace had not been understood or claimed. Salvation is where all real healing begins. Once a person has entered into a personal relationship with God through Christ, God's resources are available to combat generational iniquities.

"God Is Punishing Me"

2. *"God is punishing me for the sins of my ancestors."* Bill, a high school friend of mine, throughout his life carried feelings of false guilt and unworthiness. Bill's father was a convicted felon. The arrest, trial, and conviction brought his father income loss and shame. The distraught father eventually committed suicide. Now Bill had to carry that burden too. As a star athlete, Bill found some positive support, but the comments of others and his own thought about his father's guilt kept plaguing him. He punished himself for his father's wrong. Being numbered with the racial minority of our town probably added to Bill's burdens. Though we weren't close friends, I tried to encourage him with my supportive compliments.

I moved on in my studies after high school graduation, and Bill did too. Reports were that he was doing very well, but one day the word came. Bill, like his father, took his own life. Tragically, it appeared that he did the ultimate in punishing himself for his father's wrongful deeds.

Bill was deceived. God doesn't expect us to carry our father's sins as our own guilt. His justice is honorable. Deuteronomy 24:16 establishes a general principle for the carrying out of God's justice. "Fathers shall not be put to death for their children, nor children put to death for their fathers; each is to die for his own sin."

God's principles of justice do not permit human courts to impute ancestral guilt to children. Unless children have participated in the crime committed by a parent or grandparent, offspring are not to be punished. Similarly, personal guilt before God depends on one's own record. Judgment and eternal wrath fall upon those who have personally transgressed against God's laws. Condemnation awaits those who fail to repent and avail themselves of the mercy and forgiveness available through the blood of Christ. Such a person dies for his own sin and not that of his forbears.

Likewise the virtue, faith, and goodness of a parent does not earn salvation for a child. Each individual must make his own personal decision. Each must receive God's mercy for his own guilt through Christ's finished work. Personal accountability is an important principle in God's dealings with each human being.

Though God's general provision is to safeguard children from being punished for their parents' sins, God reserved His right of exceptions in His administration of justice. There are biblical instances where God judged even infants together with their wicked parents. The flood of Noah's day, Sodom and Gomorrah, Jericho, and the entire Canaanite culture are familiar examples. Tiny infants, children, and even animals fell under the judgment of God's justice and wrath. Later discussion will focus on why God's judgment may be that severe in such instances. At this point, we need to stress the norm in God's dealings with His own people. A forbear's wickedness will neither keep one from salvation nor make spiritual victory impossible in a Christian's life.

"God Is Unfair"

3. *"God is unjust and unfair to 'visit the iniquity of the fathers upon the children and the children's children to the third and the fourth generation.'"* Human reason struggles to understand God and His ways of administering truth and justice. It has always been that way. But when we mortals question God's justice concerning His ways, we fail to recognize our God's transcendent greatness. This side of heaven, human minds will never be able to understand all of God's workings. His administration of His justice must be left in the perfection of His wisdom and understanding.

Suffice it to say, God's ways are always just and holy. Justice, truth, and holiness are attributes of His nature and character. When we question God's ways that are clearly set forth in His Word, the problem is never His problem. God remains eternally just because justice is part of the very essence of His being.

Man proves his ignorance and the great folly of his being when he tells God how to work out His justice. There are times when we may fail to understand. Questions are legitimate. Expressing them to God gives Him respectful honor. One might state: "Lord, I don't see how this fits into Your love and mercy, but I want to. I know Your ways are always holy, just, and loving. You could not be anything else."

THOSE FOOTPRINTS IN THE CARPET

God can help those who are experiencing the outcomes of a negative delayed harvest; He responds to prayers of His people. As we will see in the next chapter, we have a God who bestows His grace though we are unworthy. That's important to know in this dark and sinful world in which we live. In the late twentieth century, drug usage, sexual perversions, occult sins, and even the open worship of Satan are rather common. With such wickedness abounding, we need to use wisely our spiritual resources to walk in spiritual freedom—and to help our children find that freedom. That's what this book is about: cultivating our children's spirits to yield a good harvest, for their well-being and for Christ's honor.

Practical, biblical truth has been placed in our hands. It must be understood and used aggressively to help parents and children walk in freedom from the hurtful damages of the "delayed harvest" now being reaped in human lives.

What an assignment we face. Only God's grace can enable us to keep it simple enough for a child to understand.

The Lord is the answer to our needs. We began this book with the story of Ted, whose "footprints in the carpet," seen by his daughter Linn, reminded her of his nightly prayers on her behalf. Let's look more closely at Ted and his wife, Chris, to understand how parents can protect their children from the wolves around them. Their story shows more completely how biblical principles can free parents' own lives and their children's lives from the harms of the delayed harvest.

Early in their marriage Ted and Chris came to our church. They had been born-anew believers for only a few years and found the spiritual food that they desired and needed was lacking in a liberal church setting. God graciously led them into our church, and we became good friends.

God began to lead Ted and Chris into a deeper understanding of faith and prayer. For six years they had longed to have a child, but conception didn't happen. It was in this crisis that Ted began to learn about faith and prayer. "I was sitting in church with the congregation," Ted says, "and I remember committing to the Lord our children that I really believed God was going to give us. I told the Lord that I would dedicate them to Him and trust Him with their future. I promised the Lord that Chris and I would do our utmost to give them the spiritual guidance and direction that they would need to grow to love and serve the Lord."

As Ted finished his prayer a great peace from God settled upon him. God did bless this couple with a daughter, Linn, and three years later, Peter was born. From the moment they learned of each conception, these parents began to pray for each child. After the birth of each child, Ted and Chris continued to pray daily over Linn and Peter. Usually the parents prayed at the child's bedtime, with each child participating as he or she grew older.

About this time Ted and I together attended a week-long evangelism conference in a distant city. Each day Ted heard me pray the doctrinal, warfare style of prayer for my family and his that God ingrained into my prayer practice. Ted related, "It was there I learned to use my authority to pray against the influence of Satan and his kingdom. This started a revolution in my prayer life, especially as it related to how I prayed for my children."

When Ted returned home, he began the practice that left his footprints in the carpet. Each night after the children were sleeping, Ted entered each child's room and prayed a warfare prayer over them. On occasion, while he prayed, they would awaken enough to hear Dad praying quietly. As they grew older, they would even kid Dad about his "long, boring prayers." Yet, they learned to respect the value of those nightly intercessions. At this writing, Linn and Peter are both attending a Christian college. Recently, they were home for a longer weekend. It was in that time that Linn came to her mother and with tears in her eyes asked, "Is Dad still going in our rooms each night to pray for us even though we are away at college?"

Linn's tears speak clearly. She was moved by her father's commitment. More important, those prayers made a difference, as Ted learned how to intercede and tap into his resources as a believer. His action suggests how we can be parents who pass on a delayed harvest of blessings. It also shows one way we can lessen the threat of a delayed harvest of sinful wrongs— through thoughtful, specific prayer. I asked Ted to reveal the type and content of his "footprints in the carpet" praying. Ted recorded for me a sample prayer, and I want to close this chapter with the transcription. Only a few repetitious phrases are omitted.

Prayers of this type are very personal, but we can learn from one another better praying. May our Lord raise up tens of thousands of dads who will have the dedication to pray like Ted does for his children.

Our great God and heavenly Father, I humbly come before You in the name of the Lord Jesus Christ. By the power of His shed blood, I claim Christ's victory over sin, Satan, and all of his principalities and powers of darkness. I ask that Satan and all his evil powers assigned against my family would be bound and rendered unable to work their wicked plans against Linn, Peter, Chris, or me. I position my family under the protective blood of my Lord Jesus Christ, and I claim all the promises You have given to us through Your Son. I claim the promise of eternal life, of salvation, and of life with You in Your eternal kingdom.

Dear God and Father of our Lord Jesus Christ, I worship You and give You thanks for all that You have done in our lives. Thank You that we can approach the great and powerful God of Abraham, Isaac, and Jacob. Thank You for the cross of Calvary, for the sacrifice of giving Your Son to die that we might live and have eternal life with You. In the name of the Lord Jesus Christ, I ask that any strongholds Satan's kingdom has established in our lives would be torn down and destroyed. I ask You to forbid that Satan or any of his demons would be able to have any effect upon

Linn, Peter, Chris, or me.

Heavenly Father, station the holy angels round about us to protect us and to keep us safe from the evil and harm that might be near. I pray that Your Holy Spirit will control fully our hearts and our lives to remind us of our kinship and sonship with You. Please focus our attention on You. Guide us with Your eye that we would be conscious that we are a part of Your forever family who always follow after You.

I pray specifically for Linn. Minister to her in a special way today. Keep Your holy hand upon her. Grant to her strength, wisdom, power, and sharpness of mind. Help her to have a spiritual hunger to seek after You. I pray, heavenly Father, for You to raise up a Christian young man who loves the Lord and would love Linn. Draw her to him and him to her at just the precise moment known in Your plan. May theirs be a happy Christian home all of their days.*

I pray the same for Peter. Raise up a Christian young woman whom he will deeply love and who will return his love with deep devotion as his helpmate. May You bless both of our children with their own children and grandchildren who will walk after God and serve You from the earliest days of their lives. Help Peter in all of his choices of life to always seek Your guidance and wisdom.

If it pleases Your will, Chris and I would like to enjoy our children's children before You call us to Yourself. I look to You to keep Your hand upon our family in all of our ways. Protect us from the wiles of Satan, the allure of the world, and the deceitfulness of sin. Please keep us surrounded with Your holy, protecting angels. Draw each one of us closer to Yourself because we pray in the name of our Lord Jesus Christ with thanksgiving. Amen.

*As this book goes to print, Linn has completed her college degree and recently married a deeply committed Christian man.

CHAPTER THREE

THE DELAYED-
HARVEST PRINCIPLE

I carry a copy of an obituary in my briefcase. It recounts the life and legacy of my great-grandfather, whom I mentioned in chapter 1. The name at the top is "William Ludwig Bubeck." Born in Germany in 1830, born anew into God's family shortly after arriving in America in 1852, he lived eighty-five full years before God took him home early in the twentieth century.

As noted earlier, Great-grandpa Bubeck's obituary contains a lengthy focus on his Christian testimony. Two sentences capture the tone of his Christian character: "He loved Christian people of all denominations, and his great soul looked upon the whole world as his Master's kingdom. He rejoiced in every movement that had for its object the establishment of that kingdom among men."

He was a man of great prayer, and my family and I are reaping a harvest of blessing because of the seeds he sowed many years ago. So keeping the obituary in my briefcase doesn't mean I'm thinking about death. I'm thinking about a life of blessing. I take the obituary out and read it at regular intervals. Though I didn't even know about him until recently, I'm still benefiting from his godly life.

FROM GRANDPARENT, TO PARENT, TO CHILD

Minta wasn't that fortunate. She came to my attention when her therapist in a distant city sent her for counsel and evaluation. Though reared in a Jewish home, her parents practiced few of the traditions of the historic Jewish faith. Minta remembers her father as a hardworking materialist who "didn't know how to show love to any of his children." She saw him as critical, bitter, and miserable in all of his associations of life. He was murdered during a robbery attempt, and Minta recalled her feelings about his brutal death. "I felt guilt—I felt guilty that I still hated him so much. He was never a part of my life when I needed him."

Her relationship to her mother was equally painful. In Minta's written evaluation of her mother, she used words like *manipulative, accusing, hateful, depressed, angry,* and *constantly complaining.* Through her mother, Minta was also introduced to fortune-telling, palm reading, and the use of the pendulum to find direction for her life.

Eventually Minta became a follower of Christ. Yet as a believer, she found her life one of infrequent joy. Minta battled most of the same character flaws that hurt her so much in her family. She struggled throughout the rearing of her own two children to not treat them as she had been treated. "I see faces, shadows, and movements all of the time when I'm alone. I have regular visits from a spirit called Mike. He tells me what to do when I'm feeling bad." Her occult exposure through her mother has opened Minta to such harassment.

Generations of unbelief, occultism, rejection, and bitterness have left deep scars in Minta's life. As she learns how to apply the truth of her faith in Christ, freedom is coming, but it's been a stressful road. Minta soon recognized the generational origins of her struggles.

"I can see this generational thing so clearly. My dad was a heartless materialist just like my grandpa. I doubt if my dad ever heard a kind word of encouragement. He treated me just like he was treated. Mom carried on the same superstitious interests that her mother followed.

"My brothers and sisters are almost as messed up as I am. I can see in all of us the same loneliness, misery, and destructive behavior that our parents and grandparents lived out."

As Minta thought about her family, insights came. Tears of relief and concern appeared. "Oh, this has got to stop! I can already see my kids struggling with some of the same feelings and low self-esteem that plagued me all my life. Our whole family has been affected."

A TALE OF TWO FAMILIES

Family blessings do seem to flow from generation to generation. I know a family of missionary, educational, and pastoral leaders I'll call the Whitemans that is now reaching into the fourth generation of godly ministry. They have reputations of sterling character lived out in faithful, godly witness. Although I've not made close, personal scrutiny of their spiritual lives, I have been close enough to enjoy some of the fragrance from their exemplary conduct and morals.

In contrast, another family that has produced Christian leaders extending through several generations tells a different story. Among the Rangels, three men in successive generations have been pastors of considerable ability, yet each has become involved in adultery while in pastoral leadership. Those moral failures led to their resignations. Three generations of moral sin that disgraced those men and their Lord's reputation. The hurt to their families, their friends, their congregations, and their own lives was a measureless tragedy. The harm done to those with whom they were involved in immoral conduct is equally disastrous.

We all know the flow of generational stories similar to those of the Whitemans and the Rangels. How do we explain them? In the past, "folk" explanations have been varied. Failures were sometimes called "bad blood." Conversely, the more desirable generational qualities were commended. I still remember hearing my parents talk of strong character coming from "good stock." Is that the explanation for what went wrong with the Rangels—poor stock, or "bad blood"? Hardly. We need to lift the theories of character development above the level of folklore and even above the debate over heredity versus environment; we need to search out the biblical implications.

THE NEED FOR RESEARCH

I believe we have neglected an important area that needs more biblical study. A better understanding of the issue of "generational transfer" could give believers more insight into some of their peculiar problems with temptations and defeats. Good biblical balance would seem to indicate the need for careful study of the issue of generational transfer. Investigative study is overdue. I would hope that some Th.D. candidate will make it the research topic for a dissertation. The Old Testament emphasis on genealogy, judgment of families and cultures, and the references to the faith and lives of men like Abraham, Isaac, and Jacob has promise of fertile study on the subject.

We must ask some questions: Are there theological insights concerning character and conduct traits passing to succeeding generations? If so, can these be both negative and positive? Does the Word of God speak to such far-reaching issues?

Surprisingly, biblical scholars have written little on this subject. Although I'm not treading on completely new ground, the lack of scholarly, biblical writing on the issue of generational transfer of sin and virtue limits comparative research. Those involved in helping believers find freedom from spiritual oppression recognize the problem. Timothy M. Warner, professor emeritus at Trinity Evangelical Divinity School, has touched on this important issue in his book *Spiritual Warfare:*

> One generation lives with the effects of the good or the bad done by the previous generation. That this has application at the personal level is readily accepted in the physical realm . . . . The

same principle applies in the spiritual area. Demons claim that if a parent was giving them ground through unconfessed sin in his or her life, they have the right to harass the offspring of that person. . . . Renunciation of the sins of parents and ancestors should be a standard part of the conversion/discipleship process.[1]

A few other authors have also acknowledged the issue in their writings,[2] but more research is needed. Christians need practical help to see how this factor fits into responsible parenting. Among Christian scholars and counselors I would like to see more studies that would help parents develop ways to guard their children from the negative aspects of generational transfer. What practices can parents institute to pass on generational blessings to their children and grandchildren?

In this chapter we want to wrestle with larger issues: What are the consequences of the sinful failures of our forefathers upon our own lives? What benefits and blessings come to me from the godly ways of my generational forbears? To answer these questions, we will open the Scriptures and deal with some doctrinal basics. This will be helpful and practical.

ORIGINAL SIN AND GOD'S GRACE

The palms of my hands were sweaty. I paced about with nervous tension. Thoughts raced through my mind: *Am I prepared enough? Is the subject too heavy for my congregation? Do I really understand the subject matter? Will I bore the people with doctrinal preaching?* Finally the deacons came into the study and we prayed. I went to the pulpit still tense but resolved to do my very best.

I well remember those first experiences of preaching expository sermons from the book of Romans. It's one thing to learn about original sin and its consequences in the academic setting of Bible college, and quite another to expound spiritual truth from God's Word. That's particularly true when preaching on the deeper subjects of original sin and redemptive grace. As a young pastor, I wondered whether the people for whom I was spiritually responsible would benefit from my efforts. Would they understand truth? Over time, thanks to God's help and that of theologians like Charles Hodge and D. Martyn Lloyd-Jones, my church audience began to understand the profound truths of original sin and God's redemptive grace. These two doctrines are highlighted by Paul in two verses in Romans 5:

> Sin entered the world through one man, and death through sin, and in this way death came to all men, because all sinned. . . . But the gift is not like the trespass. For if the many died by the trespass of the one man, how much more did God's grace and the gift that came by the grace of the one man, Jesus Christ, overflow to the many! (Romans 5:12, 15)

Those verses contain the heart message of the whole Bible. It's an astonishing declaration that confounds the minds of the best theologians. There are two major parts. First you have the declaration "that both sin and death 'entered into' the life of man and into the story of the human race as the direct result of that one man Adam's act of disobedience."[3] Guilt, condemnation, sin, and death itself came upon humanity by the sinful disobedience of the first Adam. We usually use terms like *inherited sinful nature* or *consequences of the fall* of man in theological discussion, but this is *generational transfer* with a capital *T*. Adam's sin brought the sentence of death to every human being. His guilt became our guilt.

Though it reaches in the opposite direction, the second part of the apostle's declaration is even more astonishing. To escape the spiritual death and judgment we deserve likewise depended upon the actions and grace of one man. Jesus Christ, the last Adam, removed believers from the realm of guilt, sin, and death. They enter a new realm of righteousness, joy, peace, and everlasting life. All this depends on the person and work of Jesus Christ alone. Redemption remains all of God and all of grace—grace shown by God through His Son. Spiritual salvation comes through Christ's work, and nothing can separate us from what Christ has done. The merit and worthiness of Christ is imputed to each believer. The righteousness of Christ is also credited to us, insuring justification.

Who can measure such wonder? It will be the theme of the worship and praise of the redeemed throughout eternity. That praise is expressed in Revelation 5:9–10 in all of its profound truth:

> And they sang a new song: "You are worthy to take the scroll and to open its seals, because you were slain, and with your blood you purchased men for God from every tribe and language and people and nation. You have made them to be a kingdom and priests to serve our God, and they will reign on the earth."

Christ's magnificent work to redeem lost people will cause angelic beings to enter into a chorus of praise: "Worthy is the Lamb, who was slain, to receive power and wealth and wisdom and strength and honor and glory and praise!" (Revelation 5:12).

Our guilt in Adam's original sin accomplished man's lostness. Adam's act was both sufficient to condemn us all and to establish humanity's need of salvation. Man's sinful desires are directly related to our inherited sinful nature. Likewise, our forgiveness required imputing, or transferring, another's merit to our own standing with God. The message of redeeming grace rests upon the obedience of One; the good, sinless life of Jesus Christ and His atoning death are credited to believers as their own. Though it is not commonly used in theological terminology, the thought conveyed by *transfer* is not a new theological concept.

Saving grace also imputes equal benefits to every person who believes. All receive eternal life. Each receives equal benefits upon turning from sin and trusting Christ as Savior: regeneration, justification, forgiveness of sins, peace with God, citizenship in heaven, the indwelling of the Holy Spirit, and membership in the body of Christ. These benefits are credited at the moment of saving faith. Each benefit comes from our Lord Jesus Christ. His life, His worthiness, His riches, His righteousness, and His standing before God are bestowed equally to all who receive Him as Lord and Savior.

TRANSFER OF THE FATHER'S SINS

The consequences of Adam's original sin was conveyed to every subsequent member of the human race on an equal basis.

All became equally guilty, equally condemned, equally lost, equally helpless to earn merit with God, and equally in need of this saving grace. But there is a second kind of transfer that is unequal. While Adam's sins transferred the consequences to each of us, when it comes to our own family issues—the generational transfer related to family bloodlines—there are many varied aspects. They are not so clearly defined and forcefully stated in Scripture as those just considered. We are concerned about issues represented by God's warning to Moses of His "visiting the iniquity of the fathers upon the children and the children's children to the third and fourth generation" (Exodus 34:7b, NKJV).

What It Doesn't Mean

I have heard counselees tell me, "My sufferings and sin problems are all due to the sins and failures of my ancestral lineage." As we consider how sins transfer from generation to generation, caution is in order. We cannot use our parents' sins to excuse our own. Generational transfer does not mean our sins are primarily our parents' doing or responsibility.

We must not totally blame our ancestors for our sinful choices. My friend Jim suffered from this passive, fatalistic view of himself and his struggles. He viewed himself as the helpless pawn of his genes and his family environment. It was a major breakthrough when he realized that he'd been deceived. Through redeeming grace, the truth of Scripture, and the sanctifying work of the Holy Spirit he was freed from patterns that were bringing disaster into his life.

I read with him from the prophets Ezekiel and Jeremiah. Both men declared God's rebuke for such faulty thought and theology:

> "What do you people mean by quoting this proverb about the land of Israel: 'The fathers eat sour grapes, and the children's teeth are set on edge?'
> "As surely as I live, declares the Sovereign Lord, you will no longer quote this proverb in Israel. For every living soul belongs to me, the father as well as the son—both alike belong to me. The soul who sins is the one who will die" [Ezekiel 18:2–4; see also Jeremiah 31:29–30].

Jeremiah and Ezekiel had to deal with both the natural and judicial aspects of this fatalistic proverb. It was wrong to blame the judgment God was administering as being caused by the sins of the fathers. Both the ancestral and personal guilt were worthy of God's wrath. It was equally invalid to blame one's personal bent to sin upon an inherited compulsion from a parent. The proverb echoes an excuse I still hear today: "I can't help sinning these ways because I inherited the tendency from my father."

G. Campbell Morgan summed up the proverb this way:

> If your teeth are on edge, do not blame your father. Whoso-ever eateth sour grapes, his teeth shall be set on edge. If your teeth are on edge, you have eaten the sour grapes.
>
> "Yes, but my father did eat them, and I had a tendency to sour grapes before I was born." Is that so? Then God is greater than your father, and the forces that He places at your disposal are greater than all your tendency toward sour grapes.
>
> "Yes, but I have eaten them myself. I plead guilty. God help me, I am guilty. I have eaten them. My teeth are on edge, and I have contracted a liking for sour grapes! Though I hate them, I must have them."
>
> God is greater than one's liking. Get back to Him. He will put Himself between you and your father and between you and your past, for the river of God is flowing, and there is life wher-ever the river comes.[4]

There is a relationship between the sins of a father and those of a son, but the personal accountability of each individual supersedes the transfer. "Every living soul belongs to me," God says. The father and the son is each equally accountable to God for his own sins.

What It Does Mean

Believers do well to try to understand how God visits the sins of the fathers upon the children to the third and fourth generation. Several factors need our evaluation and careful thought:

1. *A parent's sinful choices of environment and example do have far-reaching consequences upon his or her children and the children's children.* Many see the basic message of God's warning referring to the influences of the home environment. As children suffer the wounds and negatives of the failing aspects of the home and parental influence, the children carry on those negatives to the next generation.

Most would admit this as part of this sobering warning. Children reared in a climate of cursing, pornography, drug usage, immorality, or drunkenness will be wounded by any of those environmental factors. Dysfunction by parents creates a dysfunctional family. Children reared in an unhealthy climate are often conditioned to carry out the same patterns as they mature. They may hate their past home life but still be caught in its web.

2. *A parent's sinful emotional wounding and physical brutalizing have far-reaching consequences upon the children.* In chapter 1 Linn described the footprints in the carpet by a godly father. When Ted entered his children's rooms after they were asleep to pray over his daughter and son, the benefits would come later. Linn remembers those visits fondly.

Yet, tragically, such nightly visits from fathers or stepfathers are not always noble. I and other counselors hear much too often of quiet visits from a dad who took sexual advantage of his daughter or son during the night. What an abomination! Other fathers in acts of anger have verbally assaulted their children, using cutting words to belittle, ridicule, or even reject their kids. Some have struck their children in fits of rage.

The emotional wounding that comes from sexual or physical abuse can last a lifetime. Healing is long and difficult in a person's life when he or she has been exposed to such abusiveness. But of all the kinds of physical abuse, little has more devastating consequences than sexual abuse. It rips at a child's identity, esteem, security, and trust in an adult. In my judgment, only parent-authored satanic ritual abuse does more damage to the child.

These problems often transfer from one generation to another. A sexually abusive parent usually was sexually abused by some trusted family member when he was a child. Abusers produce abusers.

Dave experienced this transfer of pain. He came for counseling because of the violent anger tantrums he was experiencing toward his own children. Dave loved them deeply. It tormented him to see the fear in his children's eyes when they thought they had offended him. As we counseled, he finally admitted to me and himself that at times he felt strong sexual urges toward his son. He couldn't understand: *How can I, a Christian father, have such evil temptations toward my own son?*

Being a believer, he had successfully resisted that perversion, but the very temptation tormented him. As Dave talked openly about his torments, he was enabled to recognize that his Lord understood and wanted to help him come to freedom.

Through prayer and time, Dave eventually found forgotten memories resurfacing. They were not pleasant. Both his father and grandfather had violated him sexually. The fears, confusion, guilt, and anger from these violations had been so traumatic in Dave's childhood that he dissociated. His core person had detached from any conscious remembrance of those horrible, traumatic experiences.

Remembering was important to his own healing, but new spiritual and psychological struggles began to emerge. They proved very painful. He had to forgive a deceased grandfather and his living dad. It was not an easy struggle. Pains of this kind demand much grace and wisdom from God.

Dave worked through it all. God graced him with forgiveness and he was able to even confront his aging father in a healing manner. The anger and sexual temptations lessened. Dave was able to handle them by using the weapons of his warfare on a continuing basis. The grace of our Lord Jesus Christ does heal the sins of the fathers even when they have been deeply damaging.

3. *A parent's sinful physical vices have negative consequences on the children.* We are living in a time when much is being said by the medical community about the damage that the sins of the parents can bring to their children. Except the medical professionals don't call it sin; they call the activities *vices* or *unhealthy habits*. It doesn't matter. The outcome is the

same: damaging and often far-reaching consequences to the children. Little babies are being born addicted to crack, heroin, or some other illegal drug. A pregnant mother drinking alcohol during her pregnancy can mean both mental and physical damage to her baby. The dangers concerning a mother smoking or even being in the environment of tobacco smoke during her pregnancy are being studied carefully. The unborn may suffer detrimental consequences from such exposure.

The dangers of such unhealthy behaviors can last years. (Experts say "crack babies" remain unstable, aggressive, and hostile for as long as two years as the parent's drug affects the nervous system.) The consequences may even last a lifetime. (Ask the adult child of an alcoholic who struggles as he finds himself seeking the bottle, even though he despises his alcoholic parent for doing so.)

Much more could be written about how offspring suffer when their parents have a sexually transmitted venereal disease. New, drug-resistant strains of these diseases keep challenging the medical world's researchers.

The latest and potentially greatest health risk comes to newborn children whose parents are infected with the human immunodeficiency virus (HIV), which carries with it the risk of AIDS. The shared needles of drug abusers or sexual promiscuity often leads to HIV and AIDS, which can be passed on to the offspring during birth. AIDS remains an incurable yet largely preventable disease. To the thoughtful observer, the sins of our progenitors do have profound consequences.

How to Limit Transference

Negative generational transference can be overcome with consistent prayers and godly examples. Similarly, the lack of consistent prayers and godly living by our forbears makes our children (and us) more vulnerable to transference.

That our fathers can give a positive legacy should encourage us in seeing that sins need not be passed down. Great spiritual benefits do flow forth to children and grandchildren from the prayers and godly watchfulness of ancestors. Timothy wasn't the only son and grandson to be blessed by the faith that first lived in a mother or godly grandmother (2 Timothy 1:5).

Sadly, many people must face life with all of its complexities and temptations without the supportive prayers of godly forbears. This puts them at a terrible disadvantage. As one who has so benefited, I can only praise God for such an heritage. Only the love and grace of God can overrule the terrible lack of such heritage blessings.

THE INFLUENCE OF DEMONIZED ANCESTORS

Generational transfer of sin can come from one other source: *demonized ancestors*. This final truth is controversial; some will disagree here. But this can be a valid cause of sin transfer to our children, for sound, biblical reasons.

Most can see the validity of the generational harm from the things just mentioned, but the thought of demonic troubling passing from one generation to another is going too far. They reject it categorically. One popular Christian writer states his rejection of such possibility in these strong words:

> When God visits iniquity on three and four generations in a row, it is because each successive generation chooses to sin against God, not because their ancestors have done so.
> Nowhere in the Bible is there an example of a true believer who inherited demons from his ancestors. . . . Nowhere in the Bible is there an example of a true believer who was inhabited by demons because of transfer.[5]

The above author is concerned primarily about the issue of Christians being "inhabited" or "invaded" by demons. Yet, he seems to categorically reject the concept of demonic influence or control transferring from one generation on to a succeeding generation.

Those who hold this view argue that a good and loving God would somehow protect newborns from such a fate. In my view, such assumptions usually flow from fear of the demonic realm and the possible affliction of demonic activity. They see demonic activity as being much worse than transfer problems from cocaine, alcohol, or AIDS infection. Demonic activity is assigned a more serious level of problem than the emotional and psychological rubble the abusive actions of parents pass on to their children.

I feel that's wrong. To say that third and fourth generational consequences of sinful wrongs couldn't include something as serious as demonic troubling is to proscribe limits that are not biblical. God has not set such limits concerning the consequences of generational sin. If biological, emotional, and psychological harms flow from generation to generation, can we exclude the demonic? Just because some see it as "scary" is not a valid foundation.

This is a delicate matter. We must be careful not to imply that the sinful actions and attitudes of children always indicate demonic activity. That would be ridiculous, and it would violate biblical truth concerning the sinful nature of us all. All of us, including little children, can act very wickedly without any prompting from the kingdom of darkness. "The heart is deceitful above all things, and is desperately wicked; who can know it?" (Jeremiah 17:9, NKJV).

We must face the fact, however, that little children can be demonized. A demonization problem that proved too difficult for His disciples to handle confronted the Lord Jesus when He came down from his transfiguration (Matthew 17:14–23; Mark 9:14–29; Luke 9:37–42). In Mark's account of Jesus' conversation with the father of the victim, it was confirmed that the demonization had been a part of the son's life from "childhood." The Greek word is *paidiothen*, which could include any child from birth through the early years of a child's life. Gerhard Kittel states that this Greek word was usually used for a child below seven years of age.[6] It is the word used of the infancy of the Lord Jesus concerning His birth and dedication in the Gospel records. Both the word and its context of usage in Mark's account support the view that the child was probably an infant, at least very young, when the problem manifested. This terribly destructive demonic power had tried to destroy the man's son from infancy. How do we account for that?

If indeed he was this young, a child could not open his own life to such control by choices to participate in occult sins, immorality, idol worship, or other sins giving Satan ground. G. Campbell Morgan calls attention to the demonic problem not being related to any personal sin on the boy's part with these insightful words:

> Turning from our contemplation of the man we look at the boy. In this connection it is an arresting fact that the Lord asked the father how long the boy had been in that case. Necessarily we know that He did not need information. There was, undoubtedly, however, a reason for the enquiry, and the reason was that there should be clear understanding of how desperate a condition he was in. The father answered, "From a child," which quite literally means from his birth. Thus we see that the possession of this boy by an evil spirit, with all its terrible consequences, was not the result of his own personal sin. . . . The boy is revealed utterly beyond the reach of human efforts, suffering mentally and physically through no wrong of his own.[7]

Morgan is clear that the demonic suffering is totally removed from any "wrong of his own" on the part of the boy. There certainly is some valid explanation that has to do with truth. I believe the explanation is in the same realm of other maladies that come on children because of the sins of their progenitors. Cocaine-addicted babies were not addicted by their own wrongdoing. The mother's addiction was transferred through the physiological tie to the unborn child.

There is a generational transfer problem that extends beyond the psychological, physiological, and other bondings to our ancestors. Participation by all of Adam and Eve's progeny in the fall of humanity suggests that *spiritual consequences* in some measure are also transferred. I conclude that this is how this demonized little boy received his most hurtful condition.

My biblical study and years of counseling the demonically troubled have brought me to conclusions that I believe are biblically valid. From birth this young child probably was victimized by past generational wickedness. The family lineage door was opened. Wicked spirit activity was able to focus on the infant. It could have been a parent, grandparent, or even an aunt or uncle that opened the door for such a tragic consequence.

"This kind" (Mark 9:29) probably indicates that the degree of strength and level of authority troubling this boy were very powerful. The disciples couldn't deal with this evil spirit. The Lord Jesus advised the necessity of more prayer and even fasting for the disciples to be able to deal with the deceptive ways of such an evil spirit. If they can gain any claim, the most powerful of wicked spirits can and do trouble little children. How was the claim established?

Though no explanation is given, permit me to suggest what I consider a valid probability. Could it be that one in the child's generational heritage had been deeply into some dark, spiritistic practices? Such practices open any person's life to demonic activity and control. Even believers are warned to avoid spiritistic practices with some very strong words:

> The sacrifices of pagans are offered to demons, not to God, and I do not want you to be participants with demons. You cannot drink the cup of the Lord and the cup of demons too; you cannot have a part in both the Lord's table and the table of demons. (1 Corinthians 10:20–21)

Idol worship is demonic worship. The deeper a person gets into spiritistic activities the more he opens his life to demonic participation or "fellowship" (NKJV). What a horrible fate that is. This young child may well have had family members in his heritage who participated in the idol worship of those times. Perhaps the one giving such serious ground had died, but demons don't die. They live on and seek to continue to do the same destructive, deceiving work of darkness to some generational family member.

I believe that this area of generational transfer is an important factor in comprehending God's judgmental dealings with wicked people and wicked cultures. When God spared Nineveh to the chagrin of Jonah, one of the reasons He gave to His distressed prophet was: "But Nineveh has more than a hundred and twenty thousand people who cannot tell their right hand from their left, and many cattle as well. Should I not be concerned about that great city?" (Jonah 4:11).

Most commentators see this as a reference to the little

children of Nineveh. The repentance of the city gave God opportunity to hold back the wrath of His judgment upon the city. God was reluctant to destroy the city in judgment because of the many we might refer to as innocents. The Lord chides Jonah for not being more concerned about these. Yet, we know that God did judge cultures and wiped out every living thing in the culture. How do we explain that?

God's promises to Abraham shed some light. The Lord had promised to give the land occupied by the Canaanites to Abraham and his seed, but that seemed a long, long way off because Abraham at the time didn't have any son. It was a long way off. In Genesis 15, God told Abraham of a four-hundred-year sojourn of his descendants in Egypt. God's explanation to Abraham was short but profound: "In the fourth generation your descendants will come back here, for the sin of the Amorites has not yet reached its full measure" (Genesis 15:16).

The iniquity eventually was complete. God commanded Joshua and his armies to judge and destroy men, women, and children. I believe the fact that even the little children were to be killed has to do with the demonization of a culture. Wickedness, the worship of false gods (which Paul equated with the worship of demons—1 Corinthians 10:14–22), and the total moral degeneracy had filled the cup. The Canaanite, Amorite culture was beyond repair or continued mercy. The generational wickedness had demonized the whole culture. Men, women, and even the children must be destroyed or the demonized, generational transfer would continue on and on.

In his extensive book on spiritual warfare, Ed Murphy lists six sin areas that can lead to the demonization of believers. The first on his list has to do with generational sin.[8] C. Fred Dickason, theology professor, counselor, and expert on the occult, writes in *Demon Possession and the Christian:* "I have found this avenue of ancestral involvement to be the chief cause of demonization. Well over 95 percent of more than 400 persons I have contacted in my counseling ministry have been demonized because of their ancestors' involvement in occult and demonic activities."[9]

Those of us who are seeking to help people tormented by

demons would concur with Dickason's findings. Demonic activity does tend to follow generational lines. A large majority of the troubled people I've been able to help have a family history of occultism. The salvation wrought by our Lord Jesus Christ is sufficient to interfere with the schemes and plans of Satan's kingdom to keep the transfer of demonic control extending on from generation to generation.

COMING FREE

The redeeming power of our Lord Jesus Christ is sufficient to set the believer completely free from all generational consequences of sin. The victory of Christ and the freedom of the believer must never be in question. The believer is not only sure of eventually winning, through Christ he has already won. We remain more than conquerors because we are one with Him who has conquered.

Such great truth and reality is not to be passively assumed. The believer's walk of faith necessitates the aggressive application of our freedom. This is true in overcoming all of our enemies, including the transference of sin from generation to generation that threatens to harm our children or grandchildren. Our Lord Jesus Christ's finished work is able to protect and free us and our children from the transfer of the harmful aspects of a delayed harvest. We need to know it, pray it back to God and against evil, and live in the freedom of our faith.

The apostle Peter had deep compassion for the hurting believers who were under attack by the world, the flesh, and the Devil and his kingdom. I think he had the generational transfer issue in mind when the Holy Spirit breathed out through Peter these mighty words:

> Since you call on a Father who judges each man's work impartially, live your lives as strangers here in reverent fear. For you know that it was not with perishable things such as silver or gold that you were redeemed from the empty way of life handed down to you from your forefathers, but with the precious blood of Christ, a lamb without blemish or defect. (1 Peter 1:17–19, emphasis added)

The blood of Christ can and does remove the necessity of experiencing the delayed harvest of our forefathers' sinful practices. Yet we must not passively assume our protection. Knowing truth but not acting upon it is very dangerous. We must stand in the absolutes of God's truth as we face all of our enemies. Truth sets us free from the rule of all that opposes God's will.

The power of prayer to free us from such forces is available against *all* attacks. In my book *Overcoming the Adversary*, I relate the testimony of a woman who was attacked by seizure kinds of problems while she slept at night. The medical and psychiatric diagnosis referred to them as "anxiety attacks." They were more than that, however. I quote the pertinent part of her story:

> We discussed the possibility of Satan's involvement. Not only were the seizures painful, but they were frightening as well. We carefully considered the believer's biblical authority to refuse Satan the right to rule any area of our lives. In Romans 6 [this husband and wife] saw their privilege and responsibility to "not let sin reign in your mortal body so that you obey its evil desires" (Romans 6:12).
>
> A careful procedure was planned. The next time a seizure began, they were immediately to challenge any of Satan's involvement by forbidding him to rule in this way. We talked of how the husband could come to his wife's rescue by challenging any spirit of darkness behind the seizure. He was to say, "In the name of the Lord Jesus Christ and by the power of His blood, I resist any spirit of darkness that is trying to cause my wife to have a seizure. I forbid you to do it. I command you to leave our presence and to go where the Lord Jesus Christ sends you." He was urged to insist repeatedly until the seizure was broken. His wife was encouraged as best she was able to repeat the challenge her husband addressed against Satan.
>
> As our friends utilized this strategy, the seizures ceased completely. In this case demons had indeed been involved and were seeking to intensify a human weakness.[10]

The freeing-up process may extend over many years. The powers behind that initial attack were quickly defeated and forced to leave her life and presence. She enjoyed a good ministry of Bible teaching and Christian service of many types. Her function as a mother and wife were exemplary. Yet, as she put it, "a cloud of depression and unhappiness was always present. Though I did not understand this, I could not find anything in my life that could be contributing to the cloud. I longed to be free from it all."

After attending our Defeating Darkness conference in 1992 where MPD (multiple personality disorder) had a major focus, new insights began to come to this lady. Through the helpful encouragement of a Christian counselor, she prayed for the Lord to reveal any forgotten memories that could be key to her freedom. She asked her Lord to grant her the ability to enter into the full joy of her salvation. God heard her prayer and granted her freedom. The Lord brought her to a level of spiritual and emotional freedom that she had never known before.

What was the hindrance? What explained the clouds of darkness that were always there in the shadows of her active Christian life? Generational occultism that included sexual and satanic ritual abuse[11] had been a part of her troubled childhood of pre-conversion days. Dissociation had kept it hidden from her conscious memory for many years. As she remembered, renounced the evil, forgave her offenders, and received the loving mercy of our Lord Jesus Christ, this woman found freedom.

Generational sin and a delayed harvest of dark shadows can lift away. In Christ there is consummate freedom. A delayed harvest of such darkness, when brought to Christ, can be turned to glory.

PART TWO

HOW TO LOVE LAMBS

CHAPTER FOUR

PARENTS WHO LOVE EACH OTHER

Jennifer's eyes began filling with tears the moment she was seated. While she struggled for composure, I led us in a prayer of petition for the Lord's quieting comfort. But as Jennifer tried to explain why she had come, her body trembled under the stress of troubled emotions. She regained control and pulled a tissue from the box by her chair. Dabbing at her eyes, she poured out her story.

"I'm so ashamed. I'm finding it difficult to live with myself. I completely lost control of my anger. Rage and very nasty words poured out of me against Russ. I even threw a vase at him and it broke in a million pieces. He was yelling at me too! We were a first-class mess. What really breaks my heart is that Sammy and little Jenny saw all of this. They looked so lost and afraid."

Jennifer convulsed into uncontrolled sobs. I let her cry. Tears can be very therapeutic. As she regained control, words of repentance came pouring out. "Oh, Lord! I'm so sorry! I'm so sorry! Please forgive me and please heal the hurt of our children! They're so little and we hurt them so much." A new rush of tears and sobs accented the moment.

Touched by her sincere brokenness, my own eyes brimmed with tears. "Does Russ regret what happened as much as you do, Jennifer?" I asked. I knew bad quarrels sometimes leave lingering scars and resentments that drive people apart. They blame each other and reject personal responsibility.

Her reddened eyes quickly fastened their attention to mine. "Oh, yes! Russ feels as ashamed as I do. He can't believe how two people who love each other could be so angry and mean—especially when we're Christians! He wanted to come today, but he had to work.

"This doesn't happen too often, but when it does we blow it big time! We both saw how our anger frightened and crushed Sammy and Jenny and we know something has to change. We really need help!"

I gave a sigh of relief. The hope for change and healing held much promise for these hurting Christian parents who recognized their shortcomings and wanted to change.

"When you both know that, Jennifer, you've conquered a major hurdle," I assured her. "I'm so glad you came because I believe I can help you find that level of freedom the Lord has for you and Russ! You're wise to recognize the harmful hurt to your children, but God may well use it for good. The pain of your problem has served to motivate action. As you learn to walk in your freedom, you'll be able to teach your children to walk in theirs."

LOVE VERSUS FEAR

Children suffer deeply when the parents they love resort to abusive words and actions toward each other. Feelings of fear and guilt usually plague a child exposed to nasty, shouting exchanges between angry parents. In his confused immaturity, a child often feels he is responsible for his parents' anger. Because he loves each of them, he is unable to assign responsibility to them. The child's security, derived from his parents' love of each other, is lost. Panic takes over. Relative to the child's sensitivity level, terror and torment often replace the sense of loving security every child needs.

The inspired words of the apostle John should speak deeply to Christian parents:

> There is no fear in love. But perfect love drives out fear, because fear has to do with punishment. The one who fears is not made perfect in love. We love because he first loved us. (1 John 4:18–19)

Failure to understand the deep damage that parents' angry shouting matches place upon their children's lives is dangerous. In contrast, the inverse of that is liberating. The freedom from fear and quiet security instilled in children when their parents deeply love and respect each other sets up solid rock foundations for the family. God desires that Christian parents provide that level of security to each of their children.

It may surprise you, but the first way to love our lambs, those children whom God has given us, is to love our spouses. In doing this, we establish a foundation that steadies our children against the attack of wolves. We will look at the importance of such love shortly. But first consider John's warning later in chapter 4. Though he was writing to all believers in his first epistle, his sobering words have a special application in a Christian marriage:

> If anyone says, "I love God," yet hates his brother, he is a liar. For anyone who does not love his brother, whom he has seen, cannot love God, whom he has not seen. And he has given us this command: Whoever loves God must also love his brother. (1 John 4:20–21)

Loving your "brother" applies to husband/wife relationships. The capacity to control anger and to speak with love and respect to one's spouse is part of Christian grace. It goes with faith's "turf." The victory of our Christian walk meets its greatest test in the home. When it works there, the benefits are rich and ongoing. Everyone benefits from the security—your spouse, your children, and, of course, you. Neighbors often notice. Spiritual freedom means that we are daily learning to live out our faith, especially in the intimacy of marriage and parenting.

THE POWER OF A STRONG MARRIAGE

In these times when so many things that have great value are being discarded by society, Christians are to counterbalance this trend. The rubble of brokenness now prevailing and accepted by our secular culture must not rob the Christian family of its rightful heritage. The well-being of our children is too important. For children, the Christian faith becomes real when they can see its transforming virtues lived out by their parents. Spiritual values consistently modeled by parents communicate powerfully to children. Showing love to each other, forgiving each other, foregoing your rights to help your mate—such actions will build in your children faith and confident hope for the future.

Character values are visibly demonstrated by the best people a child knows. Biblical conduct becomes more than a set of do and don't rules. They see the patience, forgiveness, kindness, and love of Christ visibly working out in the intimacy of the home.

Loving your spouse not only makes your Christian faith appealing to your children—something that works—it also has an impact on the culture. Godliness has a long arm. Our responsibilities to be light that dispels darkness and salt that inhibits corruption are basic tenets taught by our Lord Jesus Christ.[1] When the fruit of the Spirit controls a believer's conduct and attitudes at the family level, the resulting benefits radiate out into the world scene. The difference becomes strikingly visible to those wounded by the darkness and corruption common to all sinful cultures. This is the way the Lord planned that salt and light would do their confronting, transforming work within the world system.

In his classic book, *How to Really Love Your Child*,[2] respected Christian counselor and psychiatrist Ross Campbell emphasizes that the prerequisite to effective parenting is that the parents love each other:

The most important relationship in the family is the marital relationship. It takes primacy over all others, including the parent-child relationship. Both the quality of the parent-child bond and the child's security are largely dependent on the quality of the marital bond. So you can see why it is important to assure the best possible relationship between wife and husband before seriously attempting to relate to your child in more positive ways. . . . The stronger and healthier this bond is, the fewer problems we will encounter as parents.[3]

Those good words express the thesis of this chapter. When Mom and Dad encourage and support each other, communicating love in front of the children, a balm of security clothes their children. No other factor is as important. To become a growing reality in your marriage, such love needs to be a top priority in both prayer and commitment.

But it isn't an easy proposition. Every marriage trembles at times. Modern-day tensions, the pace of living, and the decline of moral and spiritual values all blast away at a loving marital relationship. Only God's grace and deep personal commitment can enable us to provide the security of marital love for our children.

I marveled as I observed Mary and Sid, hardworking business people who seem deeply in love. Yet I knew their story: Married in their middle twenties, mature, college-educated, and committed to loving each other, they encountered severe rocky places that could have devastated their marriage. Work tensions, emotional conflicts, several moves due to changing jobs, strong personalities—all put their marital love to severe tests. They sought the help of a marriage counselor. They found direction in God's Word and times of prayer. But the key to adjusting and loving each other came from something else. I asked them to write down their "secret" one day.

Here's what Sid wrote:

The demonstration of my parents' love commitment tested through the real life encounters of their forty-plus years together is the single most influential element in my love for Mary. It's the cement that keeps my commitment glued in loving focus.

Seeing that same commitment mirrored in the marriage of my wife's parents helps me know that we can and will make it. My commitment is fixed. It's the only option!

Mary's written explanation echoed her husband's. She attributed her commitment to her own parents' "unconditional love," concluding:

> Their devotion to each other motivated my determination and prayer focus . . . [on] parental love and security. I know it's God's plan. I refuse anything less for my girls. I keep looking to my Lord for the ability to love [Sid] with the forgiving encouragement and sensitive tenderness my parents showed and my Lord has for me.

OVERCOMING A PAINFUL PAST

Sid and Mary love each other for the benefit of their children. But what if you missed the example provided by faithful, loving parents? Maybe your home life was a disaster. Are you doomed to repeat the disaster? No! As valuable as a loving parental example is, grace and mercy can overcome the worst of a dysfunctional heritage.

Josh McDowell, Christian apologist and a gifted speaker, is regarded as an exemplary husband and father. Yet his drunken father spent little time with him and occasionally beat Josh's mother. "Sometimes I'd go to the barn and find my mother lying [there] behind the cows, beaten so badly she couldn't get up. I hated my father for treating her so cruelly, and to avenge that treatment I would do everything I could to humiliate or punish him."[4]

The wounds of such a dysfunctional family could have spelled permanent disaster for Josh, but God's grace and mercy began to work. After struggling with the credibility of the Christian faith, Josh finally decided to trust Jesus Christ as his Savior. His spiritual birth brought about a gradual personal transformation. Eventually he would meet Dick Day, now one of his best friends, who also had grown up in a dysfunctional family and now had a loving marriage. Dick loved his wife, Charlotte, fully and his four children equally. Josh felt Dick was sent by God, and wrote that Dick and Charlotte "loved their kids, with affectionate words and touching—lots of hugging. You might say I learned to hug by hanging around the Day family. . . . In a real sense, Dick's family became the family I never had."[5]

The other influence for healing his wounded family came when Josh met Dottie, who now is his wife. Dottie always spoke with enthusiasm about her family; they meant everything to her. When Josh finally met Dottie's parents, he noticed the same qualities of family love he had seen modeled by his friends, Dick and Charlotte Day. From her dad, Josh began to learn "all kinds of things about what it means to be a loving husband and father. . . . He was always encouraging his kids, affirming them, and showing them he cared."[6] The healing would continue. Today Josh McDowell is enthusiastic about his family, devotes much of his spare time to his wife, and gives lots of hugs.

Being reared in a home where Mom and Dad deeply loved each other is God's best way, of course. But you can surmount even the most difficult family background, with God's help. He is a gracious God, one who can help parents victimized by a hurtful heritage to rise above a painful past. Both Josh McDowell and his friend Dick Day say that loud and clear. Providing a heritage of parental love for your children is not only desirable, you can achieve it.

HOW TO GROW LOVE IN YOUR MARRIAGE

If love between parents is so important, how can I develop it? you may wonder. There are no quick, easy steps that will produce argument-free marital happiness. One could wish that frustrating issues could be resolved that easily within Christian marriages. Though books on strengthening your marriage are helpful and I strongly recommend them,[7] reading a book does not guarantee you'll love your spouse more. Seminars, retreats, and renewal weekends also can help. Couples in troubled marriages can also find help through counseling. Yet, despite all the help available, far too many Christian marriages are being lived out in disarray. Marriage partners hurt so much that they shout

out their frustrated rages at each other or, worse yet, they take it out on the children.

When the pain gets bad enough, parents can and do resort to divorce, but the children can't do that. They have no "resort" solutions available to them. They just cry or "stuff" the hurt inside. There it festers, and with the passage of time can become explosively destructive.

I believe that when couples have marital and family needs they too often dismiss the spiritual issues in their relationship. Psychological counseling often relieves such troubled needs, but other help may be more needed. We hear that hackneyed advice: "Why don't you just pray about it?" or, "Why not take it to the Lord and let Him solve it?" Most of us recoil from such spiritualized clichés that oversimplify. Though often well meaning, counsel like that inevitably adds to the guilt and wounding of the one who is struggling.

Although such glib advice may be used to piously cloak a counselor's incompetence, we must not allow the hurt to turn us from seeking a spiritual remedy. Often the spiritual dimension holds the answer. Indeed, permanent answers to all human need can be found only in the Lord Jesus Christ.

My many years of studying the Word of God and a practical, engineer's mind (though I never trained for engineering, that's the field in which aptitude testing predicted I would excel) have combined to motivate me to develop some important spiritual essentials Christian couples need to practice. The understanding of a pastor's heart has reminded me to keep the list simple and workable. So here are some essentials for a well-ordered Christian home that are worthy of disciplined, deliberate practice. Remember, in growing your love for your mate you are practicing a key way of giving your children security—to make your lambs bold and wise as they prepare to move out of protective pastures.

The Power of Prayer

"Bill and I need to see you, but I doubt that there is much that can be done. We fight over everything. I guess we just aren't compatible."

I was surprised to hear Cathy's hopeless evaluation. I'd observed their courtship, taken them through premarital counseling, and then married them just two years ago. I had considerable confidence that they would do well together and wondered what had happened to cause such despair and hopelessness.

During our first meeting, the couple seemed to engage in a quarrel of silence. After prayer, I tried to breach the silence by asking them to make a concise statement of their problems. No big difficulties emerged. Both seemed bored with each other and bored with marriage. They even concluded a divorce would benefit Billy.

"Billy will suffer less if we have the divorce while he is still an infant. It is easier that way—easier for him and for us," Bill said.

Their calloused indifference to each other, to their child's best interests, and to their Christian witness angered me. I resorted to an approach that I have rarely used. I rebuked them sharply.

"I'm really disappointed in you both. You embarrass me! Where is that commitment love we discussed so thoroughly in the premarital counseling sessions? I think you also embarrass our Lord Jesus Christ. I know you are both saved, but you're acting as though the Lord Jesus has done nothing for you. You're despising His work and His will. You're about to break this most sacred relationship of marriage and neither of you seem to care a snap about it. You'd have to be both blind and ignorant not to know that Billy needs you both . . ."

I can't recall all that was said, but I kept the pressure on until some tears began to flow. Bill's eyes brimmed with tears first. When Cathy saw his tears, she began to sob quietly. I backed off my rebuke and quietly waited.

Bill broke the silence. "What can we do? We didn't plan it this way. It's just a lot of little things and I guess we're both spoiled and stubborn! I know a lot of it is my fault. I miss the freedom of my single days."

Before they left that day, we charted a course for rebuilding their marriage. The cornerstone for the rebuilding focused on prayer. They agreed to pray together each day for God to bless their marriage. Each was to ask the Lord for help to complement the other's needs. Each was to ask God to build into them a God-authored level of committed love that would refuse to give up their having a happy marriage.

Did it work? They are grandparents now. The greatest benefit to any marriage is the fact that God answers prayer.

If you want to learn to love your spouse, pray. Pray, asking God for the ability to see your spouse as the special gift he or she is. Pray that you would learn to practice patience, forgiveness, and love for your spouse just as God does for you. And pray with your spouse.

During my pastoral years, I had a prerequisite for counseling a couple whose marriage was in trouble. After asking if they were praying daily together for God to bless their marriage (I never received an affirmative answer), I went on to establish some parameters. If they wanted me to counsel them, they had to agree in my presence that they would daily pray together that God would strengthen their marriage. If they failed to make that commitment, I would not continue counseling.

The results still amaze me (though perhaps they shouldn't). Big problems often melted away. I sometimes received more credit for my counseling expertise than I deserved. The only real answer was that God had answered their prayers. What tragedy and trouble we bring to a marriage when we neglect the most important ingredient. How presumptuous to assume that God will bless our union without our humbly asking Him to do so.

Several kinds of prayer should be regularly practiced in a Christian marriage:

1. *Fasting prayer.* Fervency often expresses itself by fasting. The one praying desires God's intervention more than he desires food. With careful attention to health factors, there is a proper place for fasting and prayer. No Christian couple should ever resort to divorce without at least one partner caring enough to fast and pray for the Lord's intervention and healing of the broken relationship. Intervals of fasts that last one to three days over a period of time will honor the Lord and can bring miraculous answers.

2. *Daily prayer together*. Marriage is a spiritual relationship. To properly recognize this, every Christian couple needs to set apart a time where they practice this reality by prayer. Asking the Lord to enable each partner to complement the other's needs is a proper use of prayer.

One note of caution. Never use your prayer time to preach. In fact, it's best to have a rule that each will only pray for the Lord's help to make each a better marriage partner. Save your prayer about negative factors in your relationship to private prayer times. Instead, pray together for God's blessing on your marriage.

3. *Doctrinal, warfare prayers*. Couples should read together doctrinal, warfare prayers. Anita and I try to do this daily as part of our devotional time. By alternating paragraphs, we both stay attentive and alert to what we are praying. We use the kind of printed prayers that are shared in this book. Such a practice will stimulate and motivate a couple to consider the spiritual attack their marriage may be facing and remind each other of their resources in Christ.

4. *Family prayer*. "Lord, we acknowledge that everything that is good about our marriage and family has come from Your loving grace and mercy. We reach out for more and more of the goodness You have for us." Parents need to pray that way as they lead their children in family devotional times. For families to be healed, we must see daily family prayer times re-instituted.

A Biblical Approach Toward Money

The "Resources for Parents" (pages 223–25) includes readings that deal with the money issues of the Christian life. Several excellent writers are explaining biblical principles of finance. Only a few years back, such studies were not available. Money problems are a chief stress factor in many Christian marriages. A proper attitude toward money and the responsible handling of financial matters is necessary to any good marriage.

Here are three basic suggestions that reflect the biblical principle of being stewards of our resources, all of which come from God.

First, *practice percentage giving*. Financial matters in a Christian home require the first priority of a Godward focus. The benefits of tithing are many. The Lord is quickly made the focus of your finances. He receives of your increase first, even when it means personal sacrifice. He receives your praise when financial increases come. You share the burden with Him when there is not enough, knowing that He knows He is first in all financial matters. Extravagant purchases for self-gratification begin to disappear. Budgeting becomes an adventure to see how much more than the tithe God will grant to give to His work.

When you tithe, you have funds to give to worthy, needy situations. And, perhaps best of all, a Christian couple's focus is on treasures in heaven rather than earthly riches.

Anita and I were married two years before we learned that we needed to tithe. Our would-be tithe money went toward sending a "poor boy" through school. Mark Bubeck was getting a seminary education, but God wasn't blessing that self-centered focus.

A number of factors combined to show us God had a better way. Unexpected doctor bills, traffic fines, broken typewriters and you name it, left us with a balance in the red every month. Finally my wife and I had a Sunday dinner with a leading elder and his family. Once a month I preached at his little church, where thirty or less attended. I was amazed at the large offering from such a small congregation. Thirty or less—yet their offerings often totaled several hundred dollars. During the meal, I decided to ask him to explain the high offerings.

"We all tithe!" he said. "Even the children and young people give at least a tenth of their income for that week. We share testimonies of how the Lord is blessing us in our personal finances and we're all learning that you cannot out-give God."

On the way home that afternoon Anita and I talked about it. That day we began a lifetime of giving. I could write a whole book about the results of that commitment. What a joyful adventure.

Second, *develop a simple, workable budget*. Study and planning need to go into projecting a functional budget that will enable you to pay all the bills each month. I remember how shocked and surprised I was as a young pastor when I counseled a couple in their forties. To pay their bills each month they needed nearly six hundred dollars. Their total take-home income was just over four hundred dollars. If they had not been able to take out a home equity loan, financial disaster would have overtaken them. The development of a simple budget brought them both under financial discipline.

Third, a*void credit card purchases unless you are able to pay off the full bill each month*. Credit cards can ruin more than budgets. They can ruin marriages. They often force people into bankruptcy. Unpaid annual balances make you pay nearly 20 percent more for each purchase. In addition, credit cards help people develop the idolatry of greed.

Credit cards should all be required to carry the warning label: "Have been proven to be dangerous to the health of your finances, your marriage, and your emotional well-being. Use only with well-ventilated biblical sense."

Conflict and Communication

I once counseled a couple who were seeking divorce less than twelve months after their wedding day. The husband had struck her and now was devastated by guilt and shame. "I can't believe I would ever hit any woman, let alone my lovely wife!" he remonstrated, his eyes brimming with tears. "It frightens me to realize how I lost control." The wife was not sure she wanted the marriage to continue, even though the ugly bruise had almost disappeared. "Do you think you can help me, Pastor?"

What caused the blowup? As they talked, we soon uncovered a communication problem. Even during minor disagreements, they would not talk with each other. One time they quarreled over—but did not discuss—whether they would sleep with their bedroom window opened or closed. He was a macho-man type. He needed his fresh air to sleep properly. She was always cold and even having the window open a crack caused her to shiver with cold.

A power struggle developed over such a minor matter. Her mind-set was that if he really loved her he would want her to be comfortable when they slept. His frame of reference told him that if she respected his manliness, she would adjust to what had become an important practice of his life and health. That unresolved communications conflict led to a stance of marital war. She exploded when he left his dirty socks on the floor. He complained that his eggs were too hard and the toast was burned. As they drove to work, she criticized his driving. Though there were times when all seemed to be forgotten and forgiven, festering underneath a real quarrel was going on and they were losing respect for each other. Unresolved anger was building into bitterness. Finally, in a quarreling time, he struck his wife.

Many readers will recognize patterns similar to their own struggles. Communication over sensitive areas of conflict is not easy even in a good marriage where you love each other deeply. Finally, in the objectivity that the presence of a counselor introduces, this young couple found an answer. They purchased an electric blanket with dual controls. When the bride was able to keep warm enough, she actually enjoyed the fresh-air atmosphere. But the most important factor to the future of their marriage was that they learned to communicate about sensitive issues with mutual respect. That's so important.

With prayerful respect for each other's views, any Christian couple can learn to do this. It's best to schedule objective, clear-the-air times.[8]

When we give in to the rule of the fleshly sin of anger, we open the door for the evil works of darkness in our lives. If we justify our resentments and anger, if we fail to discuss with our mate sensitive areas of disagreement with respect and love, the Devil soon begins a level of ruinous rule (Ephesians 4:26–27). Communication of this nature is a spiritual matter of great urgency. Pray about it; but equally important, *do it!*

Barriers Due to a Spiritual Battle

Sometimes poor communication between a husband and wife are caused by a spiritual battle. Satan wants to disrupt marriages, especially between Christians, and his army does its utmost to build walls, barriers, and corrupted relationships between those who are one with the Lord Jesus Christ. He wants to break our communication and destroy biblical relationships so that we will blast away at each other and do Satan's destructive work toward each other. What frustration, pain, and harm we sustain unnecessarily when we do not recognize this obvious tactic. We are soon fighting each other instead of the enemy who planned it.

Carol was on the telephone with me, bemoaning how the relationship with her husband felt hindered. "It seems like there is a wall separating us. I never feel close to him any more. There seems to be an impervious barrier between us. I can communicate with everyone else but not with Tom!"

A chief strategy of war has long been to hinder, counterfeit, corrupt, or totally break the communication lines between supportive forces. Allies, generals, captains, battalions, combat patrols, and whole military divisions must maintain reliable communications or they soon may actually be shooting at each other. Satan's warfare strategy is to disrupt relationships. Carol's description of the barrier between Tom and her is an example of that strategy at work.

No spiritual truth is more important to be known and used regularly than this one. Like most great truth, the biblical answer is simple and yet wonderfully profound. We must aggressively "resist" this chief strategy of darkness on a continuing basis.

After Carol described the barriers between her husband and herself, I instructed her to start using the following resistance prayer several times each day. I had counseled her previously and she replied, "Oh, you told me that before! How did I forget so quickly? I know that really works because it worked before. I guess I was just so hurt and wounded that I forgot who was behind it. I'll get started again right away!" Here is the prayer:

In the name of the Lord Jesus Christ and by the power of His blood, I demolish and pull down all walls, barriers, and relationships being built by the powers of darkness between Tom and me. I will only accept relationships between Tom and me that are authored by the Holy Spirit in the will of God.

The fact that Carol had forgotten the prayer didn't surprise me. That's part of the Enemy's tactic too. He wants to subjectively wound us to the point that we forget to apply objective truth. When you use this resistance prayer the benefits are always at least doubled. You not only help yourself but you help your spouse, who may be unwilling or unable to fulfill such warfare responsibility. The marriage partner will, however, be able to recognize the removal of that which was hindering communication.

Attitudes Toward Sexual Intimacy

"Pastor Bubeck, I've wanted to talk to you for a long time, but I could never get up enough nerve to share my problem with you." John hesitated for a moment while he twisted in his chair in obvious discomfort. I reached out with a touch of assurance and a few words of understanding.

"I can understand that, John. I've had some things in my life at times that were so personal I couldn't quite face them, let alone share them with someone else. I know you need to talk about it, though, or you wouldn't have scheduled this time together. Please know that anything you share with me will be treated as a sacred trust in complete confidentiality. Let's pray that the Lord will give us both wisdom."

After a pause for prayer, John breathed a sigh of determination and quickly blurted out his burden. "I've had a big problem with masturbation since I was ten years old. I've never told anyone. I thought I would be over it when I married Betty, but I went back to the old habit within the first month of our marriage. I feel so guilty and ashamed. I've cried out to God to help me and I do better for a short time, but then I'm back at it. I don't know what to do, Pastor."

"Have you ever thanked the Lord for making you a sexual person, John?" I asked in the best calming tone I could muster.

"No. I'm sure I'm over-sexed. I think about sex things most of the time. Betty and I have a fairly good physical relationship together except I feel so guilty about what I do. I know if she knew she'd be really hurt. She'd feel like she was a failure when I'm the one who's all messed up!"

John's story was much like scores of others I had counseled through the years of my pastoral ministry. Sexual defeats usually cause a high level of stress in the lives of sincere Christians. Guilt feelings, self-accusations of being a "pervert," and despair of ever being able to change are the common patterns of thought.

But our attitudes and desires can become healthy as we begin to understand God's will and plan for this area of our being. Our sexuality resulted from God's creative design. He made us sexual beings and there is nothing sinful about sexual desire. It is only sinful when those desires find expression in immoral behavior patterns. Lust, fornication, adultery, homosexuality, pornography, and many other practices of sexual pervertedness trouble people. Sexual sins have many avenues, but the resolution begins when a person thanks the Lord for His plan for his sexuality.

God's will and plan for sexual expression in marriage is a highly spiritual matter. God planned it that way. The delight and intimacy of the physical union of marriage has high spiritual focus. It is meant to illustrate the intimacy and dependence that exists between Christ and His church.

Bible passages such as Ephesians 5:28–32 and 1 Corinthians 7:3–5 explain how we are to esteem the other person, demonstrating love and not withholding our bodies from our spouse, who is now part of us. Careful study of texts like these helps lift the sexual plan of God for a married couple to its proper spiritual level. It should be a focus of our prayers that the Lord might make it a "praise the Lord" time for each as His plan and blessing are lived out in the intimacy of the physical union.

Most of us come to marriage with a very polluted and corrupted approach to the sexual side of life. The world system with its sexual perverseness, the "silence" on sexuality too often practiced by Christian parents, and Satan's deliberate attempt to destroy God's plan for sexual expression in marriage have combined to hinder the spiritual focus of the sexual union. Correction of that requires prayer and the reading of Christian literature that maintains a healthy, biblical focus on marital intimacy. Spiritual warfare prayer that resists and forbids any demonic corrupting of the marital relationship is often necessary. There is no area of our lives where Satan desires to exert influence more than this one. I think it is because these evil forces want to destroy or corrupt in any way they can what God planned to illustrate the intimacy between the Lord Jesus Christ and His church. Remember, your sexual union in marriage is a spiritual matter. Make it a sacred part of your prayer life.

Other Ways to Increase Marital Love

Here are four other ways to increase the love level in your marriage. They can help you display more effectively love for your mate.

1. *Daily bestow verbalized blessings.* Beyond saying a simple thank you, we need to learn to commend our mates for good deeds, proper attitudes, and loving help.

Sometimes we may hesitate to express our gratefulness, thinking the hearer may feel proud; or we may say little because, after all, they did a common thing like clean the house, shop for food, or mow the lawn. But verbalizing our approval strengthens a relationship. Notice even the apostle Paul was a commender. All of his epistles are full of commending words. The book of Philemon is even filled with commendation for a runaway slave and a Christian slave owner who was just learning about the wrongness of such practices for a Christian. Think about words to commend your spouse. Choose your words carefully and then *say them.*

2. *Practice the touch of communication.* Touching communicates love. From the moment of birth the cuddling and touching by the mother and father communicate tender, loving care. Hugs, sitting on a parent's or grandparent's lap, affectionate pats and touches are important avenues communicating love throughout a child's life.[9] As adults, our appreciation for affectionate touch is no less.

"I love it when you come up to me, put your arm around my waist and hug me." My wife said that to me just this week. After forty-five years of marriage, we still love to be touched in a nonsexual way. Frequently when one of us awakens in the night we will reach out and touch the hand or shoulder of each other. Without a word being spoken the touch says, "I love you; you're important to me; I need to know you are near me."

Touching and caressing are important to the love act of marriage, but don't forget that simple touches on the shoulder, back, and arm, without any sexual motivation, also convey in a genuine and powerful way the love you feel.

3. *Ask forgiveness when you need to.* I cannot remember ever being closer to Anita than when I had to ask her forgiveness for some sin or failure of mine against her. I know she would say the same about those moments when she felt constrained to do the same toward me. Those are emotional times, but they are also spiritual times.

Reverence for God, love for your spouse, humility of heart, and deep spiritual ministry are communicated in those moments. Asking forgiveness is a spiritual necessity of a healthy Christian marriage.

4. *Make deliberate choices to please your spouse.* Was there anything more distasteful to the incarnate Son of God than the cross? It touched His perfection and holiness more painfully than any other aspect of His work of redemption. Anticipation of it caused Him to sweat drops of blood in the Garden of Gethsemane. The revulsion His holy character experienced at the cross was more than human vocabulary can accommodate.

A major part of the beauty of the cross to believers relates to the cost it represents that Christ was willing to pay for our redemption. The spiritual message of Christ's love that comes to us through the cross is measureless. Though it was painful and repulsive to His holy character, there was nothing that could turn Him aside from going to the cross. Because of love, He did it for us.

The intimacy and oneness of marriage is enhanced by this aspect of the message of the cross. A spouse needs to do things and go places that are not his favorite things. They might even cause you to feel revulsed at the very thought of them. How many times a wife may shiver by her husband's side at a football game when it's the last place on earth she would personally choose. Yet, there she is because she wants to do what pleases his tastes. Or how often a husband may go to a symphony concert, an opera, or some charity banquet that is of first interest to his wife. Personal choice would never get him there, but he goes and seeks to enjoy it just because he knows it will please his life mate. Such actions when done with pleasantness and good will are a spiritual ministry.

THE ROLE OF COMMITMENT
IN LOVING YOUR SPOUSE

Biblical love is commitment love. Agape love embraces those who don't want to be loved. This kind of love in marriage eliminates the word *divorce* from the Christian's marital vocabulary. Marriage really is "for better or for worse." Divorce is not a considered option. Commitment love transcends divorce.

Please do not misunderstand. Commitment love does not mean that you will just hunker down and endure a miserable marriage no matter how bad it becomes. Commitment love does not mean you cloak yourself in a martyr's attitude of suffering and pain. It does mean that no matter how bad the marriage becomes, you will maintain prayer, hope, effort, and sacrifice to make it work. Even if separation and drastic survival efforts are necessary, the commitment remains intact.

Doug and Terri had a broken marriage. Doug had betrayed their wedding vows and Terri had ordered him out of the house. Though that drastic action necessitated the sale of their home and a relocation in another city, Terri was convinced it was the only thing to do. Counseling sessions and promises of change on Doug's part had not been lived out. Serious deceptions, involvement with others, and unaccounted-for expenditures proved too much for Terri. The hurt, anger, and confused frustration brought her to the point where forced separation seemed her only hope of survival. Though young children were involved, both parents seemed to know that they couldn't live together even for the sake of the children. They needed some breathing space.

Doug got a job in another city and began intensive counseling

with a Christian therapist both he and Terri trusted. The shock
of his loss brought a degree of sobering reality into his life he
had never known. He was determined to find some spiritual
answers for areas of defeat he'd never been able to handle.

Terri and the children moved in with her parents. She
sought employment and began to make a new life for herself
and her children. Her hurt, anger, and fear made any talk about
reconciliation totally off-limits. She couldn't bear the thought
of having her trust in Doug and his word betrayed again. She
was ready for a long-term separation, though divorce was not
an option. She'd been counseled to know that divorce is never
really an answer. Not only would it hurt the children, she
understood that the Lord doesn't permit it. Terri's commitment
to her Christian concept of the marriage vows ruled out
divorce. Unless Doug sought a divorce, they would remain married but separated.

Months passed. Hope for reconciliation was slim; their
occasional phone conversations usually ended with Terri vent-
ing her hurt and rage at Doug. The passing of time did provide
a catharsis of rest and calm from all the turbulence, but talk of
reconciliation was not allowed to surface.

The context of commitment love proved to be the one
point of hope for their broken marriage. Both had opportunity
for other personal involvements, but commitment love protected each from allowing that to happen. Though the subject of
divorce was discussed once or twice, Doug also had been counseled not to seek such an avenue. Neither treated it as an
option. Though they had no answer for their frustrated and
broken marriage, they both remained committed. With the
passing of time and much prayerful intercession by Christian
parents and friends, the grace of the Lord restored their marriage. Marital counseling, patience, and commitment love had
worked. They have gone on to build a strong and well-adjusted
relationship. Their children are growing up in a restored home
with the love and support of both parents.

One of the major tragedies of "easy divorce" is the way it
helps to trample commitment love. When hurt, betrayal, and
anger are fresh, people are often vulnerable to seek revengeful

answers. The resulting rubble includes not only the marriage partners who will never fully recover from the betrayal of their vows, but also wounded children who will bear the scars throughout life.

Romantic love has an important place in marriage, but without commitment love to back it up the romance will soon prove inadequate. Romantic love is feeling-centered. Commitment love involves both the mind and the will. Christians know commitment is also a spiritual grace. Commitment love is God love. For Christian marriage, it is a spiritual necessity.

THE SPIRITUAL NECESSITIES OF MARRIAGE

Growing love in your marriage requires that we remember and practice the ten spiritual necessities to marriage presented in this chapter. They are:

1. Pray together daily for God to bless your marriage.

2. Read, work, and pray toward a biblical approach to money.

3. Keep smooth communication flowing concerning conflicts and interpersonal relationships.

4. Give high spiritual priority to the sexual fulfillment of the marital union as planned by God.

5. Use your spiritual authority to remove barriers, walls, and relationships being built by powers of darkness.

6. Bestow at least one verbalized blessing upon your spouse each day.

7. Practice the nonsexual touching of your spouse several times each day.

8. Ask your spouse for forgiveness when you need to.

9. Regularly do something your spouse likes to do that he or she knows is not your favorite thing.

10. Practice "commitment love" on such a level that your spouse is getting the message.

PARENTS WHO COMMUNICATE

He had tears in his eyes. I'd seen it only twice before. The first time was as my father spanked me at age eleven. It was only the second time he ever spanked me. I'd disobeyed him after very clear instructions in a matter that put my little brother in great danger. My dad folded the strap and laid it on the part of the anatomy suited for such correction. My cries of pain were more emotional than physical. As the discipline ended, I looked at Dad. Tears were streaming down his cheeks.

Communication. I never forgot. In those tears he told me he loved me, and what he did in correcting me was as painful to him as to me.

The second time was just before America entered World War II. December 7, 1941, was Pearl Harbor day. Like every U.S. citizen that day, a thirteen-year-old boy was greatly moved. I listened to every news report. What did it all mean? Looking for reassurance and comfort, I edged close to Dad. He was standing, looking out our backyard window. I edged around until I could look up at his eyes. He was crying.

Communication. I never forgot. In those tears he expressed his compassion and his care for our country and its soldiers. In those tears he expressed concern that his sons might be called to fight in the war.

Now his tears would flow once more. My dad and I had just placed the last bag of my belongings in the car. Our borrowed truck carried the rest of our possessions. My bride of eleven months was by my side. We were headed toward seminary eight hundred miles away. It was time to say good-bye, and Anita and I hugged and kissed Mom through all of her tears. She shed them often in emotional moments. I went to Dad. He had his back turned, looking in our overflowing car trunk. I held out my hand to Dad. As he turned and looked his son in the eye to say good-bye, tears were streaming from his eyes.

Communication! The third time in twenty years. I knew how much he cared.

Yes, my dad's caring love was deeply personal. He'd always do the hard, nasty things that sometimes need to be done on the farm. He wouldn't let his sons do those. Dad was like that too in things of danger; he did those things. His communication was so personal. He gave himself. He showed by his actions his commitment to the family and to values he believed in.

And that's another way parents rear strong children who can confront the wolves of the world. Mom and Dad can instruct by their words and deeds—by what they say and do. In their actions and words, parents teach about love and devotion that bring to their children a sense of right and wrong and a sense of security in a wayward world.

TALK ABOUT GOD'S PRINCIPLES

Anita and I recently opened a family devotional guide that asked us to read Deuteronomy 6:1–9. In Deuteronomy 6 Moses commands the people of Israel to follow the statutes and laws God gave Moses. I was arrested anew by God's admonition that parents transfer His principles to the next generation:

> These commandments that I give to you today are to be upon
> your hearts. Impress them on your children. Talk about them
> when you sit at home and when you walk along the road, when
> you lie down and when you get up (Deuteronomy 6:6–7).

But this time, as my wife read these words, a new biblical
insight flashed into my mind, all about communication. How
strongly God urges upon His people that they must communicate to their children. As parents, we must first get the truth of
God into our own hearts; then it must flow outward. We parents are to saturate our children with the communication of
God's truth. Diligent communication is to be the focus.

Deuteronomy 6:6–7 puts the communication of God's
truth at the zenith of our teaching plan. Our total conversational time with our children should skillfully relate to conveying
God's truth. While we're sitting in our homes, taking a leisurely
stroll, retiring at night, or getting up in the morning, our children are to be learning God's truth. Our words and lives must
communicate.

The home-schooling of children is becoming increasingly
popular among Christian parents. When this practice first
started, I favored the Christian school or even the secular
school over home-schooling. My view has made a 180-degree
change. Home-schooling, when done well, represents a profound improvement in education in this century. Even when it
is done poorly, in my judgment there is much benefit.

The major benefit is communication. *Parents are forced
out of their silence.* They are forced by the curriculum to talk
with their children about important, meaningful things. Profound good comes out of that. A closeness between child and
parent begins to take place that is woefully missing in this day
of television addiction.

EXPRESS YOUR LOVE

But communication is vital in all areas, not just in our children's training. It affects relationships and, when it is tender and

warm, will build trust, hope, and love among family members. Conversely, ignoring communication opportunities will hurt relationships and the parents' ability to prepare their children for adulthood.

The Barnharts were running into problems with their twelve-year-old son. Tommy was showing marks of rebellion at school and at home. Alarmed, the parents asked me as their pastor to please talk to Tommy to see if I could get through to him. Tommy and I had always had a good relationship together. He loved to be around me. He would sometimes seem to hang back as I greeted people after the service, seemingly to catch my eye and get some special attention. He seemed particularly responsive to my giving him a hug. I was eager to do what I could to help the hurting situation and an appointment was made.

When Tommy came into my office, he was sullen and withdrawn. He didn't want to talk. He seemed resentful that Mom and Dad had "ratted" about him to me. I told him how much our friendship had meant to me and that I had looked forward to those hugs each week at the door of the church. I told him that I'd missed them of late. A tear trickled from Tommy's eye. I waited.

Suddenly, brokenhearted sobs erupted from deep inside. A torrent of confusion, hurt, and anger tumbled out. I found out that at the core of Tommy's problem was a lack of meaningful communication between him and his parents. I was surprised. It was obvious to me and nearly everyone else that Fred and Nancy Barnhart loved Tommy very much. Their sun rose and set in their love for their children. I got that message from them but Tommy hadn't.

Why? Because Dad didn't show his love, and Mom did not declare her love. Fred never hugged Tommy. That didn't seem manly to Fred. Dad would watch his ball games but never complimented him. Instead, Dad always told Tommy how he could have done it better. Meanwhile, Mom never congratulated her son when his grades were good; but if they were not so good, he really heard about it. So went the scenario.

It was the old story of well-meaning parents not being able to communicate with a sensitive son. A few important apologies and some corrected communication approaches transformed a situation headed for serious problems. A willingness to change gave the whole family a new perspective.

If we are to pass on good transfers to our children and grandchildren, loving communication must be happening. There are several important areas where this needs to be taking place.

TWO KEY AREAS OF COMMUNICATION

Sexuality

Jim had a problem. He desired explicit pornography and at times engaged in fetish-associated masturbation. His marriage was in shambles. Though a believer, his sexual obsessions were destroying any witness. What was wrong? Like many men, Jim grew up not hearing one word from his parents about the facts of life. His parents never let the word *sex* escape from their lips. Neither Dad nor Mom breathed a word to him about his sexual feelings. As a result, Jim got lots of misinformation and also got a wrong impression—that sex is something you can't talk about and is a mysterious and powerful force a man tries to control.

Some may think this a strange place to begin when talking about areas of communication. I believe it to be the most tragically neglected area of communication between Christian parents and their children.

Our sexuality is one of God's noblest gifts to each of us. No one should dispute that statement. Our sexuality is God's plan. He specifically made us to be male and female. Our sexuality in the bonds of marriage is the means by which God blesses us with children and families. Our sexuality was planned by God to enable married couples to express intimacy, delightful gratification, and a oneness of union in body, soul, and spirit. When the apostle Paul was given a human experience by the Holy Spirit that would illustrate the close intimacy of Christ to the church and the church to its Lord, it should be no surprise that sexuality in marriage was chosen (Ephesians 5:21–23).

In my pastoral years of premarital counseling, more than 90 percent of those counseled said they had never received any meaningful information about their sexuality from either parent. Those who did were indeed rare. I tried to correct that tragedy, but I must admit without much success. The graded teaching materials available in our family resource center didn't get nearly the usage they deserved. I'm convinced that the perverted attitudes toward our sexuality are directly related to this abysmal lack of communication in such a vital area between parents and their children. Jim's problem started here.

In some cases, a child is rebuffed when he tries to talk to his parents about this powerful human drive of sexual feelings. Can you imagine what it says when his parents refuse to give him information? Or worse yet, give misinformation or a terse, embarrassed answer? The child quickly learns that this whole thing of sex must be very dirty business. "The best people I know can't talk to me about it." And so, instead of learning the beauty of God's plan from his parents, Johnny receives distorted and incomplete information from peers or secular, humanist educational instructors.

Fortunately, the opposite is also true. Parents who carefully plan to talk to their child can offer a healthy view of his or her sexuality. Their discussion can become an ideal time to introduce the child to biblical materials concerning sexual needs, graded to the specific child's level.

Such communication is essential. The wolves are out, and one of their tactics in shearing our lambs of strength is to distort human sexuality. Advertisers, the entertainment media, homosexual activists, and pornographers exploit and pervert sexuality for their own gain. Meanwhile, dangerous perverts and violent abusers abound in our culture. Protecting and preparing children to face this serious problem begin with regular, open communication with a Christian perspective. (See the resources under "Communicating Biblical Sexual Values," p. 224; begin to use them *now*.)

One of the Devil's chief strategies revolves around the corrupting and perverting of human sexuality. I believe he has two major purposes. The first is to dishonor the Lord Jesus Christ and His redemptive work. Satan knows that our sexual union in the bonds of marriage is meant to illustrate the love of Christ for His church and the loving submission of the church to her Lord.

The more perverted confusion and sin Satan and his kingdom can foster in the sexual area of human life, the more clouded and distorted the message of beauty becomes.

Satan's other major purpose in perverting sexuality is to create an open door of opportunity to demonize people, bringing them under demonic influence. That second purpose may surprise you. But in 1 Corinthians 6, the Lord gives us insight into why sexual union outside marriage and other forms of sexual immorality must be resisted at all cost:

> The body is not meant for sexual immorality, but for the Lord, and the Lord for the body. Do you not know that your bodies are members of Christ himself? Shall I then take the members of Christ and unite them with a prostitute? Never! Do you not know that he who unites himself with a prostitute is one with her in body? For it is said, "The two will become one flesh."
>
> Flee from sexual immorality. All other sins a man commits are outside his body, but he who sins sexually sins against his own body. (1 Corinthians 6:13b, 15–16, 18)

In the sexual union of a man and woman, a God-authored oneness occurs. Two people become "one flesh." A melding togetherness happens that can have far-reaching consequences. Among other things, this bonding oneness surely includes the opening of one's life to the demonic powers that may have active claim against the other person. Thus Satan has another means to have his demonic forces influence people. I believe this bonding involves both homosexual and heterosexual sins. This may well be the major reason God pronounced such severe judgment on sexual sins under His law. It also may provide insight into why the Lord forbade intermarriage of His people with those of heathen, idolatrous cultures. (See Deuteronomy 7:3–6.)

Of course, the most carefully taught children may make their own decisions to ignore a parent's communication about sexuality. That may happen, but it is not the usual response. Many Christian parents who have discussed the value and specialness of sexuality have watched their children guard their virginity until marriage. Without such biblical teaching, children are more vulnerable to the siren calls of pleasure for a season; many will be overwhelmed by the subtle, and not so subtle, sexual temptations offered by our wicked culture.

Spiritual Salvation

One other communication topic can lead your children to a stronghold to resist the world's wolves. Talk with them about their spiritual needs in natural yet direct ways. Parents need to watch over their children's spiritual needs and give them opportunities to respond to Christ's call.

Look for opportunities for each child to make a personal decision to receive the Lord Jesus Christ as personal Savior. Pray. But do not hit your child over the head with his need. Show tact and have biblical understanding. Remember, the Holy Spirit will do His work in each child's life. Parental teaching is in order, but not parental persuasion. We must look to God to draw our child to salvation. We do not want to manipulate by parental pressure a decision that is not genuine. New birth is not effected by parental efforts. New birth requires Holy Spirit-authored regeneration.

I remember a boy whose parents prayed but did not badger their son about his spiritual lostness. They gave all their children, in fact, consistent teaching about the need of new birth. Sunday school, vacation Bible school (VBS), evangelistic preaching, summer camp, and church attendance were part of a regular menu. For this eight-year-old boy, the Lord used VBS to lead him to repent.

He was a mischievous, fun-loving kid. Serious thoughts about spiritual needs were not top priority. Softball or some other competitive game was much more appealing. Yet the gospel message and the Holy Spirit's power were at work. On the final day of vacation Bible school, the two teachers gave a public invitation to receive Christ as Savior. That one-room schoolhouse became as quiet as a cathedral. Several girls went forward but no boys.

The eight-year-old boy struggled. Yes, the eight-year-old was I. God was drawing me. My heart was pounding. Conviction was personal and deep. I stood up and walked to the front. A marvelous lifting away of guilt and an inner peace flooded into my person. I knew something wonderful had happened to me. When I told my mother, she was pleased but also surprised, knowing I had walked down a church aisle a year earlier.[1]

Genuine conversion does make everything new. I lived out my share of sins and failures after conversion, but that new-birth life made such a difference. Parents must remember that as they pray and watch over their children. A personal salvation experience that is genuine is an essential way we prepare our children for the adult world. It should be a primary part of parenting communication.

HOW TO SAY "I LOVE YOU"

Communicating that you care on a personal level gives much security and builds healthy self-esteem. At the Bubeck household, my wife and I compose a new poem every year for each of our nine grandchildren. They get their poem from "Grandma and Grandpa Bubeck" on their birthday. They are part of a family tradition I began when I was a much younger father.

When my own children were very young, I searched for a way that I could communicate my caring love for each in a very personal way. God led me to write original poetry. Each child received her own poem on her birthday. Today every immediate family member—my wife, three daughters, three sons-in-law, and nine grandchildren—enjoys reading these personal poems. That means a lot of personal poems each year, but the rewards make the effort seem small. In my poems, I seek to communicate the truths of God as well as my own caring love. Thus, in my 1995 poem to Christie, the final two stanzas ended:

Happy, Happy Birthday! To our Christie precious pearl!
Though you may be growing fast you're still our little girl
Who's won our hearts with your love and happy little face, . . .

Lord, do keep our little Christie for many birthdays more,
And bless her with all good things from Your blessings store;
Keep her humble in her beauty and gracious in her ways,

Fill her heart with strong faith and teach her as she prays
To be like Jesus as she grows in maturity and grace
Until He comes again and we see His blessed face!

How do *you* communicate your love to your children?
There are many ways to do that. You may not be a poet, but saying "I love you" can take other creative forms. In some way,
your children need to hear that message on a regular basis.
Healthy emotional and spiritual well-being requires that we
express our love.

Listed below are my ideas for communicating of caring
love to younger children. You may want to use several of these;
develop your own list and carry through by putting them into
use as a regular practice. (In Appendix 3 you will find listings of
ideas for older children.)

Saying "I Love You" to Preschool Age Children

Here are ten ways to say "I love you" to children who are
preschool age:

1. Hug and touch in appropriate ways.
2. Express words of love and interest on the child's level of
   comprehension.
3. Read to your one- to four-year-olds while holding them
   in your lap.
4. Play games with your preschool child on her level; let
   her win some of the time.
5. Give birthday cards and parties that single out each
   child as special.
6. Pray short but meaningful prayers in his hearing which
   communicate caring intercession.
7. Do special things with each child that he loves.
8. Talk eyeball-to-eyeball with each on a regular basis.
9. Tell each child that she looks nice and is nice. Commend often; criticize never about self-worth.
10. Watch for ways to communicate caring love within the

personality traits and gifts of each child. Each child's uniqueness needs recognition and honor.

Saying "I Love You" to Grade School Age Children

Here are ten ways to say "I love you" to children who are in grade school (ages five to twelve):

1. Hug and touch in appropriate ways. Guard against touches that could be interpreted as sexual in nature.
2. Read to them books of interest on their level. Bible story books are great. Younger children love lap security, which communicates closeness.
3. Show great interest in what each is doing in school and other areas, such as sports and hobbies.
4. Let each hear you verbalize often, "I love you, Mary! You're special to me." Or "I love you, Jack. I think you're the greatest."
5. Go shopping or on a special outing with each child occasionally. This shows individual importance.
6. Listen to any emotional problems and hurts with friends and playmates. Help him learn how to respond in a biblical way.
7. Help your child with difficult school assignments that are threatening to him.
8. Let your child hear your prayers for her. At times, pray aloud about such things as what God would have her do as a life work, and that He would keep for her the one He knows would be best for her in marriage. They may overhear and realize that your love for them extends to remembering them in your prayers.
9. Honor in unique ways each one's special days. Show great concern and interest in the spiritual concerns and needs of each child.
10. Keep eye contact whenever you listen to them and when you give instructions.

LOVE AND THE PLACE
OF DISCIPLINE AND DUTY

"Don't hold back on the mower, Luke. Let it do the work. You just guide it where it's supposed to go. That's better. You're doing great." These were my words as I spent the better part of an hour helping my ten-year-old grandson learn how to mow the lawn. He wasn't a fast learner. In fact, it was a real effort for him to pay attention and learn to follow the mower in the most simple pattern. I was in a hurry to get back to my writing. I was tempted to stop the lesson and do the mowing myself. I needed the exercise and this lesson was taking too much time. In my hurrying, I almost forgot a most basic essential of communication: Patience.

I'm glad the Lord made patience one of the evidences of a Spirit-filled life. I asked the Holy Spirit to put His patience within my mind, will, and emotions in that moment. I was able to finish the session and some good communication flowed between my grandson and me.

When we administer discipline with care and oversee assigned duties, we are communicating love at a life-enriching level. It's one of the ways our Lord communicates His love to believers: "The Lord disciplines those he loves" (Hebrews 12: 5; cf. vv. 5–13). Proper words and actions of discipline communicate deep love. They tell your child you really care.

Take time to tell your child what's right and what's wrong; parents remain the major communicators of values. Don't be afraid to strongly express those values, and make your child accountable for his actions. Family counselors sometimes call this "tough love"—the kind that corrects wrong conduct and lets a child learn from his mistakes. Crying, anger, and even painful loss may result, but later the child will thank you. Discipline is a major key toward unlocking the door to your child's maturity.

Proper discipline of children requires careful thought, time, and an abundance of patience. Teaching responsibility requires both instruction and accountability. Values typically transfer to children when the parents instruct and then hold the children accountable. If children don't learn to be responsible and accountable under the patient tutelage of parents, disastrous irresponsibility may become a lifelong plague.

When I was six, Dad assigned me the task of milking a certain cow both morning and night. He often checked to see if I'd done it well. The only way I could miss my task was illness. When I did a good job, Dad commended and encouraged me. A poor job almost always meant Dad calling me back to the barn to do it right.

That was the pattern of life for my father. He pushed his sons to their capacities. I know that there were many times he could have chosen to do it himself. He could do it better and more quickly, but he understood his role to teach discipline and accountability to his sons. Throughout life, we've been grateful. That's where we each learned a hard work ethic of independence and accountability. It has served each of us well in our life assignments.

Talk to your children about having duties and being responsible. Then hold them to it. Your schedule may be disrupted as you have to check up and occasionally call them back to clean their rooms a second time (or finish milking the cow), but you will prepare them to become mature adults whom others can count on.

TALKING ABOUT HARMFUL INFLUENCES

Judy, our youngest daughter, suffered severe panic attacks as a young girl. As recounted in my first book, *The Adversary*, Judy's symptoms peaked at age eleven, with nausea and colitis creating pain, fear, and confusion. We visited doctors, but no physical cure could be found. It seemed a psychosomatic illness, and we considered counseling for Judy. But eventually my wife and I suspected a spiritual battle was the cause. With Judy's permission, we dealt directly with the powers of darkness who were oppressing our daughter (and seeking to undermine my ministry). The result was a sweet release and an immediate deliverance.[2]

Today Judy and her husband Rick are the capable parents

of our two youngest grandchildren. Now they're using spiritual warfare principles to guard their marriage and rear their children. These were learned in past struggles like these mentioned. Every trial is a learning and growing opportunity.

Judy's trial reminded me of this need to communicate with our children about avoiding harmful influences. Several years after Judy had found freedom from her nausea and panic, she shared with me some very significant information. Prior to those attacks Judy had participated with slumber party friends in spiritistic experimentation. Levitation, a crude séance, a Ouija® board, and some other mystical things like ESP were attempted. This happened when she was age eight or nine. Her attack came shortly after this occult influence.

Parents must remember that harmful influences threaten to undermine our children's growth into mature and secure adults. We need to talk with our children about harmful influences; to not do so is to not care and show our love. We need not lecture; in fact, we must use tact, godly wisdom, and biblical insight as we communicate. In the urgent times in which we live, we need to know and explain to our children the influences that threaten their well-being. The wolves out there are many; for Judy it was the occult. Other wolves who wish to influence our children include certain types of music, movies and other media, and peer pressures. Let's look at each of these.

Spiritistic and Occult Influences

You may be surprised that our Judy, as a young daughter of a pastor and spiritual counselor, had played with a Ouija board and participated in a séance. But we had not warned her to avoid such things. My wife and I were just learning ourselves about the dangers of occultism. We never dreamed that we'd need to be concerned about our protected, innocent, youngest daughter. How wrong we were!

Another of our daughters had done similar experimentation in her childhood and early youth before we'd warned her of the dangers of such things. Both daughters later experienced considerable pain that resulted from their "innocent" curiosity.

Although God taught us all so much from the results of

those dabblings, I deeply regret my ignorance of not knowing enough to warn them before it happened. Today, the influences of spiritism, far from subsiding, have exploded. Many shades of spiritism overshadow "New Age" thinking in books and movies; they invade textbooks and curriculum, even children's toys. Spiritistic influences are in music and most media; indeed, almost everywhere you look. Christian parents must communicate about the dangers of these things. We dare not leave our children in ignorance. Too much is at stake.

What is a proper approach to such issues? How does a concerned parent communicate adequate warning?

The Bible contains the best answer to meet this need. Let the Word of God express its own warning. Plan a time when you can talk separately with each child. Inform him and her of the presence of spiritistic messages. Explain how the seeming innocence and even playfulness of such things as ghosts, witches, and the supernatural actually mask the true dangers of these phenomena. This will provide opportunity for good dialogue as well as learning important information. At that point, you may want to look at Scripture with your child. A great learning text would be Deuteronomy 18:9–12 (NKJV):

> When you come into the land which the Lord your God is giving you, you shall not learn to follow the abominations of those nations. There shall not be found among you anyone who makes his son or his daughter pass through the fire, or one who practices witchcraft, or a soothsayer, or one who interprets omens, or a sorcerer, or one who conjures spells, or a medium, or a spiritist, or one who calls up the dead. For all who do these things are an abomination to the Lord, and because of these abominations the Lord your God drives them out from before you.

This passage is direct and has sufficient strength to remove any doubt that such things are dangerously wrong. You may want to look up the various words in a dictionary, such as *sorcerer* or *abominations*, to give your child the modern interpretation, while a Bible dictionary will give biblical insight. The broad, inclusive warning of Deuteronomy 18 should remove most questions about the modern-day dabblings being done by so many.

New Testament insight should be added by using a text like Ephesians 5:6–13:

> Because of such things God's wrath comes on those who are disobedient. Therefore do not be partners with them.
> For you were once darkness, but now you are light in the Lord. Live as children of light. . . . Have nothing to do with the fruitless deeds of darkness, but rather expose them. For it is shameful even to mention what the disobedient do in secret. But everything exposed by the light becomes visible. (Ephesians 5:6b–8, 11–13)

A child gains the advantage when he knows why he avoids the spiritism of the day. If he knows a text like the Deuteronomy passage, all he needs to do is read it to those pressuring him. It's very difficult to dispute with such a direct word from God. A study about the dark spiritism of Artemis of the Ephesians would help to shed light on where such spiritism always leads.

Media Influences

By definition, the media are channels that communicate information. As such, they are tools that can be used for good, conveying information, entertainment, and building a sense of community. However, that does not mean they are neutral or always used for good. What information to include and how to present (interpret) it is determined by those who control the media, whether producers, advertisers, editors, or writers. Their perspectives color the information we receive. Thus as parents we need to both monitor and discuss content with our children.

The pressures of Congress and the public have convinced the television broadcasting industry to allow the so-called V-chip to be added to TV sets to protect what our children see. This computer chip will help parents to limit the broadcast of shows with high levels of violence and sex. The need for such a chip and the TV industry's willingness to develop criteria demonstrate how even secular agencies recognize the influence of TV programming among the young.

As parents, we must communicate our love by telling our children about these media influences and helping them to discern the wolves that threaten to devour their innocence as children growing into adults. Here are two areas to talk about.

Music Influences. Our purpose here is not to debate or rehash the arguments concerning the various styles and beats of music. Much good information is available. The issue here is communication. There is sufficient evil present in the lyrics, the performers' lifestyles, and the general seductive influences in the "rock" music world to open doors for bondage to many kinds of sin. Again, the public and the recording industry have recognized the danger with a rating system that discloses the nature of the lyrics. But that does not exempt parents from their duties to help children evaluate the music they hear.

Parents must start while their children are young enough to influence, to communicate with good supportive information concerning their position.[3] We dare not wait until our children are locked into listening to some harmful music to mold their views and change their habits. Music can be an inspiring friend or a very dark enemy in the lives of children and youth. Parents must lead the way in making it an uplifting, inspiring friend that honors God.

Movies, Television, and Cartoons. When it comes to television programs, all children need parental, protective communication and supervision. Though there is some good fare on PBS and occasionally on other TV networks, most children's programs feature slapstick violence, graphic realism, and even semi-adult plots. Monsters, witches, ghosts, aliens, and other occult figures fly across the landscape. Saturday morning cartoons are no longer the innocent domain of Bugs Bunny, Mighty Mouse, or Muppet Babies. The more indulgent our culture becomes, the more parents must exercise protective oversight. Fear is to Satan's kingdom what faith is to God's. It activates evil and spiritual harm.

Again, the movie industry has adopted a rating code, yet parents sometimes ignore them; even G and PG movies can contain references to New Age thinking (the *Star Wars* trilogy) or make parents look like fools and kids wise and independent (the *Home Alone* series). And if you have a videocassette recorder or cable TV, your child has an even greater access to movies. How will you monitor them?

Here are several guidelines to help you and your children consider the shows they may watch:

- Does the fare offered promote fear, bad language, or disrespect for authority?
- Are there supernatural themes and actions displayed that are unbiblical and fanciful?
- Does the fare tend to desensitize concerning death, bloodshed, and respect for life?
- Does the viewing present an unbiblical view of sexuality, respect for parents, and spiritual values?
- Are occultism, magic, séances, sorcery, witchcraft, and other spiritistic themes presented favorably?
- Is the Christian faith held in respectful esteem by the fare presented?
- Will what's presented promote love, joy, peace, patience, gentleness, meekness, faithfulness, and self-control as desirable virtues?

Public School Curriculum

In a pluralistic society that has become afraid to teach values and tells children to decide for themselves, value-free education has only recently come under attack, as the public has begun to call for the teaching of moral values in our schools. Meanwhile certain public school systems have introduced New Age and spiritistic approaches to relaxation and learning techniques. Reading textbooks have added stories featuring witches and the occult. In my grandson's classroom in Iowa a curriculum called "Talented and Gifted" has led elementary-school-aged children into meditation in which children are told to "totally empty your mind of all distractions" and to "Watch now for someone who is coming to help you. Let him lead you."

What can Christian parents do with such reality beginning to invade the secular, public school system? A Christian school or home-schooling may be an answer. That does not work for everyone, however. Finances, abilities, and time limitations may necessitate public school for many Christian parents.

Here are four guidelines worthy of consideration:

- Communicate and keep in touch by carefully listening to your children's reports on school life.
- Keep a good flow of communication with your child, asking about and responding to ideas presented in the classroom. That way you will be able to maintain the major teaching role in your child's life.
- Teach your children to recognize the errors being promoted by the public school on evolution, moral permissiveness, prayer opposition, and humanism.
- Be an active parent in every appropriate way to influence public school decisions. That includes telling school officials and teachers about practices you deem detrimental to your children.

Peer Pressure

Peer pressure is one of life's very real pains. The desire to be liked and accepted is most basic. One way to make your children less vulnerable to the pressure to please others their age is to talk to them about who they are and remind them of your love. But it won't always work. For some sensitive children, the need to please can result in continual trauma. And the resulting conflict can be major: The child wants to conform to the accepted standards of peers and desires to please his parents. Much parental understanding is needed here.

Peers, especially children's peers, can be very cruel. Al had an abnormal fear of worms and snakes when he was a child. Now as an adult, his aversion is severe: A sidewalk worm after a rain can send him running in the opposite direction. Rage and anger accompany the panic attacks. There is a reason.

As a boy, Al was vulnerable to peer pressure. He always wanted to please and be accepted. His vulnerability made him the object of pranks and humiliation by his boyhood peers. On one occasion, they dug a hole in the woods, filled it with worms and small snakes. Luring Al to the woods on a false pretext, they had great "fun" throwing him in the hole just to hear his screams of terror.

It still makes me angry to relate that account. I do so to remind us of how ruthless peer pressure can be. Some of life's greatest cruelties happen on playgrounds. If anything should convince us of the depravity caused by the Fall, it's the cruelty little children often display toward each other.

Peer pressure is serious business. Be very understanding of that with your children and youth. Knowing that their parents know and understand the peer pressures of a child's life communicates at a deep level. Here are some specific ways you can talk to your children about peer pressure and help them be able to stand against the crowd:

- Tell true stories of the rewards of standing alone in your beliefs. Let them see the virtues of courage and sacrifice for what you believe. Bible stories, such as those of Daniel and his three friends, communicate well on this issue. Other true stories from contemporary life can promote this virtue.

- Talk with your children about the issues of peer pressure often at all ages of the growing-up process.

- Pray about the issues privately and in the children's hearing. When your child tells you about an experience when he was teased for not going along with his friends, don't dismiss it with "Well, that's them, and you should just ignore their words." Instead, take time to praise him for his stand. Ask him how he feels and *listen*. Then pray with him that God would continue to give him the courage to stand for what is right.

I began this chapter describing my dad's tears, which communicated clearly his love for people and for me. You can communicate just as clearly your love for your children. And it doesn't require shedding big tears. It only requires your having a genuine love and expressing it to your children in the midst of the issues of their young lives.

Such communication also reflects God's communication with us. Remember, we really learned the message that God is love when He became one of us. We heard as Jesus healed the sick, cleansed the lepers, wept at Lazarus's tomb, and raised the dead to life. But it wasn't until they lifted Him up on the cross at Golgotha's hill that each of us really understood: "God really loves me. He took the hard place I deserved. He paid for my sins. He rose again to fill me with resurrection life. He communicated!" And He still does. Through the saving grace of our Lord Jesus Christ there is life and hope for all who believe.

CHAPTER SIX

FREEING OUR CHILDREN

Why are you reading this book? Perhaps you're a parent with a problem child, and you're wondering if you and your spouse are reaping a "delayed harvest." Or maybe you're a new Christian, saved out of a life of darkness and sin, and you're wondering if it's safe to have a family.

It may be that you and your spouse have tried to have a family but so far have been unsuccessful. You want to adopt a child, but question whether it's safe to rear a child in this world. Or maybe you're a Christian worker—pastor, Sunday school teacher, counselor, evangelist—and you want to know better how to help people whose children are breaking their hearts. You want to help them avoid that "delayed harvest" and lead their children into a life of spiritual victory, fulfillment, and freedom.

Let me assure you: God knows all about your needs, fears, and limitations, and He is abundantly able to provide the wisdom and understanding you need. "It is for freedom that Christ has set us free" (Galatians 5:1a). It's God's will that His people walk in freedom. Not in fear and defeat. The answer is to know our past and use our present resources in Christ.

JEFF'S FAMILY

Bob and Vera Florence were concerned, just as you may be. Their sons were showing problem signs; especially their older son, Jeff. He was a strong-willed child. Fiercely independent, Jeff was determined in almost everything to have his own way. Lars was being influenced by his older brother and was also beginning to show rebellion.

The Florences' pastor advocated strong, physical discipline. He was convinced that the firm application of the rod could repair any child's problem of disobedience. Following his counsel, these godly parents demanded obedience with threats and sometimes the application of painful spankings. Lars was responding well, but Jeff was nearing nine and he responded differently. Rage, bitterness, even words of hate for his parents accompanied most of the spankings. Things were getting out of hand and they were worried. They wondered if their son might go to the school counselor and shout "child abuse!"

Having read one of my books on spiritual warfare, the Florences sought my counsel. On the information form Vera revealed that she had been introduced to the Ouija board, palm reading, and other occult and magic practices. Saved while in college, both Bob and Vera had long since put all of that kind of thing behind them. Both were deeply committed to serving Christ. They were teachers and leaders in their church, but Jeff's problems made them wonder if they were worthy to continue their Christian service.

Vera's information form also revealed another cause for concern. Her mother had maintained a lifetime interest in the mystical, magical realm of the supernatural. A professing Christian, she was interested in only "white magic." Vera's mother believed these "good spirits" she contacted were from God and He wanted her to gain their assistance to protect and help people. In addition, she was very active in the New Age movement. Reading Vera's description, I knew that her mother was also a victim of one of Satan's most clever ploys. Many like her do not realize that all such activities come from the same source of darkness and evil.

I was convinced the Florences should consider the spiritual ramifications of a grandparent engaging in such activities. Jeff's negative behavior—especially the hate, rage, and cursing at them—hinted of possible demonic control. Jeff had received Christ as his Savior at about seven. For a time his behavior had improved, but he soon fell back into the growing patterns of rebellion. These were not constant fare, but if he was denied some activity he really wanted to do, explosive rage seemed to always follow. "It's like something takes control of him!" Bob lamented.

The results that followed the aggressive practice of protective spiritual warfare would indicate that Bob's comment was on target. Powers of darkness were indeed attempting to control and dictate Jeff's behavior responses.

The remedy steps they used were very simple. God's victory is never complicated to put into practice. Most of what they did was carried out in directed doctrinal prayer. They learned to use their authority to protect those for whom God had made them responsible.

Bob and Vera began to follow three major steps that transformed their parenting and turned Jeff around. First, they began to resist and forbid any transfer of wicked spirit powers to Jeff on the basis of the ground the grandmother was giving. Two or three times each day as they went about their duties, they would use their protective authority in a prayer of this type: "In the name of my Lord Jesus Christ and by the power of His blood, I break all relationships and claims that the kingdom of darkness is focusing upon Jeff because of the ground being given by his grandmother. I ask my Lord Jesus Christ to sever and break all transfer claim that the kingdom of darkness is trying to effect to gain any measure of control over Jeff, and I ask the Lord Jesus to set Jeff apart only for Himself."

The second step had to do with teaching Jeff to deal with

his flesh and how to resist Satan's work in his daily walk with the Lord. The major focus of this chapter is devoted to communicating such teaching. Children can and will begin to walk in their freedom as wise parents teach them how.

The third necessity was to pray and plan for the turning of the grandmother from such harmful practices. I asked them to arrange for a conference session where we could sit down with her and them to discuss the needs of Jeff. She knew of her grandson's behavior problems and had much interest in his well-being. Knowing her strong personality and commitment to her views, Vera was reluctant but after much prayer, God worked it out. Such involvement is important. When those in our immediate family lineage are living a lifestyle that is giving much ground to the powers of darkness, a continuing renunciation of transfer claim should be protectively affirmed. Parents, grandparents, siblings, or even uncles or aunts should be considered.[1]

Vera's mother came for a family visit, and she agreed to talk with me on a Sunday afternoon. With kindness but firmness, I introduced her to what the Bible has to say about the consequences of getting into spiritistic practices. Passages like Deuteronomy 7:25–26 and 18:9–13 shocked her. She had no idea the Bible contained such plain words of warning concerning what she was doing. At the same time, the warnings of Exodus 20:5; 34:7 and Deuteronomy 5:9 aroused some anger. She was deeply threatened at the suggestion that her chosen interest in spiritistic practices might be causing problems in her beloved grandson's life.

I didn't press the issue. We had prayer for Jeff and asked the Lord to help his grandmother to consider these warnings of Scripture about consequences of certain sins to the third and fourth generation.

Though this confrontation of truth within the family created initial anger and barriers of communication, time has changed that. Although they do not know whether the grandmother has renounced these former practices, Bob and Vera have noted the disappearance of spiritistic literature and devices from her home. The communication now is better than ever and Jeff is continuing to walk in his freedom. As he moves into those vulnerable teen years, his parents maintain their protective stance of watchful prayer.

WHO WE ARE

I'm often amazed by the struggle elicited when counselees wrestle with the question "Who are you?" Many people don't really know who they are. No one has helped them face the depth of such a question. Some think they know but they really don't. I've often had counseling dialogues of this nature as I attempt to help hurting people:

"Who are you?"

"I'm Nancy Rogers of Kansas City."

"No, that's your name and where you live, but who are you?"

"I'm married to David Rogers; I have two children and I teach the third grade at Parker School."

"You've given me the name of your husband, the number of children you have, and what you do, but who *are* you?"

Who you are is foundational. It's the cornerstone to even begin to understand the meanings and functions of life. Parents who desire to see a harvest of blessing coming forth from their children's lives will do well to instill into their children biblical answers as to who they are.

As a parent, are you sure of your own worth? When you are, you should be able to convey to your child *his* own personal worth. Each of us should understand our value in God's sight.

A brief but profound biblical insight concerning who you are could be stated this way: "I am a person who has been created in the image and likeness of God." The dignity conveyed and the wonder invoked by that statement of truth ought not be missed by any human being. Especially your children. They need to learn it from you.

To help facilitate such teaching, I present the following outline. Some of the outline came from my own mentor and friend of many years, Victor Matthews, retired professor of theology at Grand Rapids Baptist Seminary.

WHO ARE YOU?

I. A person made in the image of God. (Genesis 1:26–27)
   A. God-granted authority. (Genesis 1:26)
   B. God-granted blessings. (Genesis 1:28–30)

II. A person of value and dignity. (Genesis 2:15–25)

   A. Our value is equal. We were all created by God as persons.

   B. Personhood communicates dignity. God always treats us as persons. He never says, "Hey, you."

III. As persons we inherited a sinful condition from the fall of man. (Genesis 3:1–13)

   A. To be sinful means you accept and believe error. (Psalm 19:12; Hebrews 3:10.)

   B. To be sinful means you practice error. (Romans 3:9–18, 23; James 1:13–16; John 8:33–34; 1 John 3:4; James 5:20)

   C. To be sinful means you inherited a nature that wants to sin. (Romans 5:12–21; Galatians 5:17–21; Colossians 3:5–8.)

IV. Redeemed persons are lifted above fallen condemnation and are of great value.

   A. They are spiritual persons. (John 3:6; 1Peter 2:9–10)

   B. They are holy persons. (1 Corinthians 1:2; Colossians 3:12; Hebrews 10:10, 14)

   C. They are gifted persons. (Ephesians 4:7; Romans 12:6–8)

   D. They are valuable persons. (Colossians 3:12; Romans 5:8; Isaiah 43:1, 4)

   E. They are persons loved and graced by God. (John 15:9–10; 17:23)

   F. They are chosen for important service. (1 Peter 2:5–9)

Our Outward and Inward Beings

Yes, God has made us valuable, Scripture says. But the Bible also notes that we as individuals have gone our own independent ways. Before we see how this has affected our relationship with God and how it affects our children, we need to understand how God has put us together. I follow a "tripartite" view of man's personhood. This theological view holds that each person is composed of three unique parts, body, soul, and spirit. An alternative view argues that each person has only a body and soul.[2] Though both views agree that each person has an outward part that we see, the physical body, they disagree about the unseen parts of our person.

I believe the Scriptures mention two unseen parts. Although there are numerous times when both unseen parts appear to be included when either the soul or spirit are mentioned, evidence remains to show a unique difference between the two, spirit and soul (see 1 Thessalonians 5:23 and Hebrews 4:12). I find it helpful to diagram those two parts as shown in Figure 1. The diagram is especially helpful when seeking to understand what happened to man at the Fall:

Figure 1
MAN AS GOD CREATED HIM

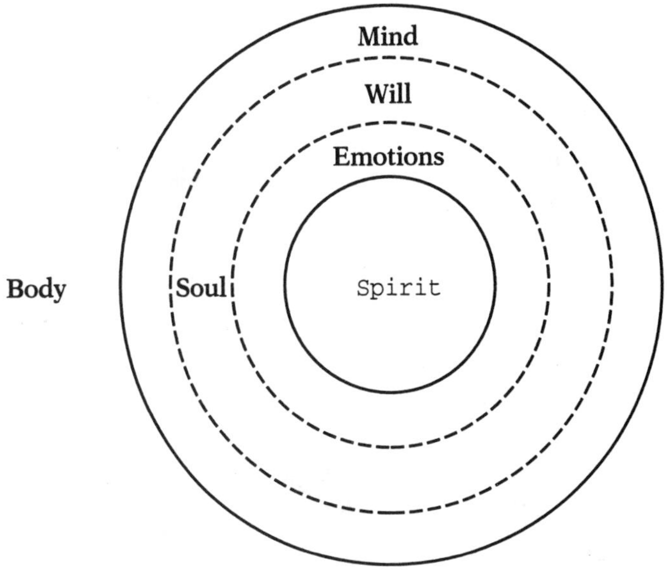

DOCTRINE THAT CHANGES US

At this point let's consider the doctrine of man and soteriology (how God has saved mankind, delivering man and woman from sin's wrath through Christ). For some, this is review; for other readers this may be new; but for all of us it is important—for ourselves and our children.

Doctrine is important. Doctrinal truth is not just the stuff we learn in church or Sunday school. Doctrinal truth is something we are to live every day. The freedom and joy of the Christian's spiritual life is wed to this premise. Freedom demands praying and living out God's truth. Victorious freedom comes from knowing and applying doctrinal truth on a moment-by-moment basis.

The Disaster of the Fall

God's original creation of man was one of perfection. The *body* was perfect in all of its parts and functions. Aging, disease, and death were not present in the perfection of the human bodies God gave to Adam and Eve.

Likewise the *soul*, where human personality resides, had no flaws. The *mind* could assimilate and understand any and all truth. It could think, reason, and understand without flaw or hindrance. The *emotions* were free from such hindrances as sadness, depression, loneliness, and fear. The *will* was also free to make choices without coercion or external control. The corruption of evil desires in no way flawed the body, mind, will, or emotions of man in his created perfection.

Man's *spirit* was that part of his perfect person that enabled him to have communion and fellowship with God. With his spirit he could know God, obey God, and enjoy the intimate, relational, joyful light that comes from perfect communion with the Lord. Innocence and righteousness prevailed.

Man's free will did harbor the possibility of disaster. God had left it so. The test focused on one tree in the Garden of Eden: "You are free to eat from any tree in the garden: but you must not eat from the tree of the knowledge of good and evil, for when you eat of it you will surely die" (Genesis 2:16b–17).

Under the deceptive power of Satan's lies and despite their pure innocence, those first persons of the human race used their free wills to disobey. First Eve and then Adam chose to ignore God's warning. Each ate of the tree and each died. We need to dwell here because what happened has great significance in understanding the principle behind the delayed harvest.

What concerning Adam and Eve died that day? Certainly their bodies didn't die. The sentence of death and the corruption of death entered their bodies, but Adam lived on for at least nine hundred years (Genesis 5:4). Their souls didn't die. They could still think, feel, and decide on actions as is evidenced by their responses to what they had done by sewing fig leaves together and trying to hide from God. They not only knew the difference between good and evil but death manifested itself in their souls by evil desires. The mind could think evil thoughts, the emotions could feel evil desires, and the will could make evil choices. The soul could still function, but it carried the sentence of death in sinful desires. Innocence was gone. (See Figure 2.)

I believe the part of man's person that died that day was the spirit. It had been created to know God, to obey God, and to commune with God in His righteousness and true holiness. Now death had come. I do not say that the spirit of man ceased to be. It ceased to function. There was no spiritual life to enable it to function.

Figure 2
MAN AFTER THE FALL

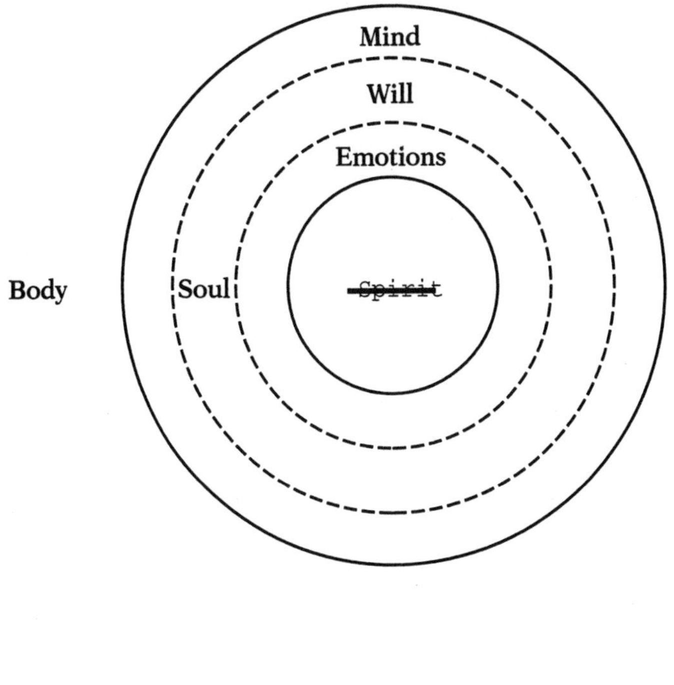

I liken it to what happens to a human body when it dies. At the funeral, we see the body of the deceased. It looks like the body of the person who died. Of Lazarus' body, Jesus asked, "Where have you laid him?" (John 11:34). The dead body was still "him" even though it had no life and could not function. The life that enabled it to function was no longer there.

I believe that is what happened to man's spirit the day the Fall happened. It died. It had no life to function. Like Lazarus's body it remains part of the person, but without the life of true righteousness and holiness necessary for the Spirit to function.

The New Life of Spiritual Birth

The earthly life of our Lord Jesus Christ introduced the plan of God whereby the disasters of the fall of mankind would be reversed. Theologically we call it *redemption*. Redemption removes fallen man's lostness and restores him fully to his God.

This necessitated *regeneration*. That which was dead must be restored to life. In His earthly life the Lord Jesus Christ gave definitive statements that shed much light upon His redeeming work. John 3:6 is one such definitive statement: "Flesh gives birth to flesh, but the Spirit gives birth to spirit."

Try to think of the significance this definitive declaration gives to your own person. The first statement tells how the results of the Fall came to each of us. "Flesh gives birth to flesh." Your flesh came to you from your biological progenitors, or your bloodline parents. From them you received your body and your soul. I've come to appreciate this more since being a grandparent. I remember when our first granddaughter started to walk. She carried her elbows slightly behind her back. I recall exclaiming, "She looks just like my dad when she walks!" Genetic physical and behavioral characteristics pass on from generation to generation.

This resemblance also shows up in the mind, will, and emotions of our progeny. Mental, emotional, and willful characteristics transfer to us from our "flesh" lineage. In 1964 my wife and I took a ministry trip to Britain. During our stay, I was able to meet a great-aunt. She had been married to my great-uncle, John. We had never met either of them. She came to one of our meetings and knew me immediately. "When I saw you walking down the church aisle, I thought my John had returned to life as a much younger man. Especially your hands look just like his," my great-aunt exclaimed. We spent several days together and she frequently remarked that the similarities were more than physical. My emotional responses, attitudes, and reasoning style were like my uncle John's, though we had never met. "Flesh gives birth to flesh . . ."

I believe this definitive statement of our Lord also tells us where the fleshly desires and temptations that come from our fallen nature will have their center of activity. Bodily appetites and "soulish" thoughts, emotions and willful actions will be the focus of fleshly temptations.

The second part of the definitive statement of John 3:6 is equally important: ". . . but the Spirit gives birth to spirit." God's plan for the redemption of fallen humanity required regeneration and new birth for the wholeness of man. This statement tells us where it begins. The spirit of man, which has no life because of the Fall, by the Holy Spirit's regenerative work comes to life at the moment of conversion. A spiritual birth takes place. As diagrammed in Figure 3, the Holy Spirit permanently unites with man's spirit.

The believer's new birth or spiritual birth is an awesome work of grace. Ephesians 4:24 indicates that the rebirth results in a ". . . new man which was created according to God, in true righteousness and holiness" (NKJV).

This statement contains a wonderful truth. Although the reborn human spirit will continue to be perfected in its knowledge and understanding, its righteousness and holiness remain a completed accomplishment of rebirth grace. Every reborn person has an inner spirit where the Holy Spirit dwells that is truly righteous and holy.

That is not true of our soul. Even after regeneration has come to a believer, the mind, will, and emotions of a person has to go through a lifetime process of "growing in grace." This work of sanctification goes on throughout the lifetime of the believer. Daily, moment by moment, the believer must yield himself to the sanctifying ministry of the Holy Spirit in order to

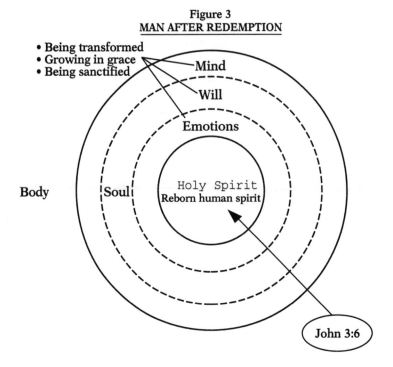

Figure 3
MAN AFTER REDEMPTION

function with righteous thoughts, feelings, and actions. This growth in grace goes on until the Lord returns or until the believer dies. To "be absent from the body and to be present with the Lord" (2 Corinthians 5:8, NKJV) seems to indicate that both soul and spirit depart and are united in completion with the Lord's righteousness and holiness. Until that eventful day, each believer will have to deal with the wicked and sinful capacities of the corrupted soul.

The body of the redeemed also must both enter and function within the total righteousness and holiness of God. This does not happen at death. The body decays into dust or burns into the ashes of cremation. Yet, at our Lord's return resurrection happens, and each believer lives in a renewed body, as the apostle Paul described in Philippians 3:20–21.

An Outline of the Impact of the Fall and Redemption

Here, in outline form, is the outcome of our lives after the

Fall and after the redemption that God provided through Jesus Christ:

MAN AFTER THE FALL

I. Consequences on the external part (the body).

   A. Receives the judgment sentence of eventual physical death with all of death's consequent expressions.

   B. Susceptible to pain, toil, disease, and various afflictions and sufferings.

   C. Able to use all of its senses and capacities to serve self, sin, and Satan.

   D. Doomed to eventually die, decay, and return to the physical elements of its creation.

II. Consequences on the internal parts.

   A. The soul maintains a corrupted personality in identity with God. Seems to have assumed the internal actions and decisions God originally assigned to the *spirit* of man:

      1. Intellect: able to receive, use, and evaluate knowledge to do one's own will and to decide one's own religion. Cannot know or please God.

      2. Will: now corrupted to serve the interests, appetites, and desires of self, sin, and Satan. Unable to choose or will to do God's will. Is held in the bondage of Satan's deceptions.

      3. Emotions: now corrupted to experience feelings of anger, hate, love, fear, peace, etc., that flow from self, sin, and Satan's deceptive rule.

   B. The Spirit died immediately at the moment of the fall of man and no longer is able to function:

      1. No capacity to know God, obey Him, or commune with Him in a pleasing manner.

      2. Unable to worship God in spirit and truth.

      3. Correct spiritual understanding of God no longer possible unless spirit is restored to life.

MAN'S REDEMPTION: A NEW BIRTH

I. Consequences on the external part (the body).

    A. What is new?

        1. Receives the first breath of the quickening life of the Holy Spirit's presence as a deposit guaranteeing its eventual glorification. (Ephesians 1:14)

        2. Is able to function in a manner that serves and pleases God. (Romans 6:11–14)

        3. Is made a "holy" body by the saving work of grace and the indwelling presence of the Holy Spirit. (Romans 12:1–2)

    B. What remains from the Fall?

        1. Still has the appetites and desires corrupted by the Fall.

        2. Still suffers pain, disease, weakness, and the defects that will eventuate in physical death.

        3. Becomes a focus point the "flesh" will use to create desire for sinful acts and thoughts.

II. Consequences on the internal parts.

    A. The soul can renew a personal relationship with God in a way that pleases Him, though a fallen nature can interrupt this fellowship.

        1. What is new?

            a. An intellect renewed by the Holy Spirit's work to receive, evaluate, and use knowledge of truth to serve and glorify God.

            b. A will with renewed capacities under the Holy Spirit's control to choose and act in decisions that will please and glorify God.

            c. Emotions with the renewed capacity to receive and live out the fruit of the Spirit.

        2. What remains from the Fall?

            a. An intellect with fallen desires still present, which may cause the mind to make choices to please the sinful appetites of the "flesh" rather than please God.

      b. A will that can decide to give in to the corrupt desires of the "flesh" that are sinful.

      c. Emotions that still have capacities to feel and experience the depraved desires inherited from the Fall.

      d. A soul still subject to making fleshly choices that produces a chastened, lukewarm Christian life.

  B. The spirit is restored to life, righteousness, and true holiness by the regenerating, indwelling work of the Holy Spirit.

    1. Able to be the channel for the Holy Spirit to bring renewing life and control to the wholeness of the redeemed person's mind, will, and emotions.

    2. Through the Holy Spirit, able to make righteous choices to obey and serve God in His will and plan.

    3. Through the Spirit, able to love God and to fulfill the desire to worship and know God.

FACING OUR SPIRITUAL ENEMIES

Many Christians blame all their problems on the Devil. Is that proper thinking? According to the apostle James, some of our struggles do come from our spiritual enemy.

As the leading elder of the Jerusalem church, James, our Lord's half brother, felt great responsibility for some of his Jewish convert parishioners who were "scattered abroad." The revival fervor of the early movement of the Holy Spirit was subsiding somewhat and the problems of living the Christian life in a pagan world were evident. On a very practical level, the book of James deals with the believer's problem areas. In James 3 the apostle compares a so-called wisdom that produces "bitter envy and selfish ambition" with wisdom from heaven that is "pure . . . peace-loving, considerate, submissive, full of mercy and good fruit" (vv. 13–17).

James declares that the false wisdom comes from one of three sources. It's earthly or of this world; it's sensual or from fleshly appetites; or it is devilish or demonic (v. 15).

In James 4:1–10, the apostle presents these three enemies in the order in which believers need to deal with them. Though they interface and work together, each is unique and requires a proper biblical approach to deal with its particular pattern of temptation. Within ourselves is the *internal enemy* that causes fights, wars, lust, murders, and can even corrupt our prayers (James 4:1–3). Prayers that flow from a selfish motive don't receive answers from God. This internal enemy is the flesh, that sinful potential for doing evil that we inherited from the fall of man. They are "desires" that battle within us. We must be able to deal with its internalized power.

Two Spiritual Enemies: The World and the Devil

The external enemy, called the *world*, tries to make believers its friend (4:4–6). Choosing the world makes us an enemy of God. Believers are warned that they have capacities to be God's enemy at least for a season of time.

The final enemy is supernatural evil (James 4:7–10). Believers are commanded to "resist the devil." Scriptural imperatives such as "submit to God," "draw near to God," and "humble yourselves in the sight of the Lord," make clear that when we are in proper attitude to Him, our problems with "infernal evil" will be minimal.

A call for a clean break with sin in James 4:8–9 conveys a clear message: "Wash your hands, you sinners, and purify your hearts, you double-minded. Grieve, mourn and wail! Change your laughter to mourning and your joy to gloom." The Lord is not against joy and rejoicing. He commands us to rejoice often in His word. The point at issue is unresolved sin. If we have that in our lives, it is exceedingly serious. It's time to deal with sin on the level of earnestness conveyed by these lamenting words. The Devil will soon have a believer in his grip if he excuses sin and fails to walk in freedom over sin's rule.

The Devil uses every arena of the world to threaten our spirit and soul. With his help, such seemingly innocent worlds as fashion, finance, entertainment, and even religion can turn us from God toward our own self-advancement.[3] The concluding outlines on our spiritual enemies should receive attentive study. The defeat of God's will and plan for believers to walk in their freedom results when our foes defeat us. Parents who desire to walk in their freedom and to teach their children to do so should make a prayerful study of these outlines.

Outlines on Our Spiritual Enemies

REDEEMED MAN FACING HIS ENEMY THE WORLD

I. The nature of the enemy.

    A. The world is an external enemy that puts pressure on the believer to conform to its value system.

        1. It is a philosophy. One Greek word for world, *aion*, appears more than forty times in most English translations of the New Testament. This word refers more to the attitude, teaching, or prevailing philosophy of the culture in which a believer lives. (Romans 12:1–3; 2 Corinthians 4:4)

        2. It is an organized system. The Greek word *kosmos* is translated "world" in most English translations more than 160 times. This word focuses on the organized structure and system of function in the world. (James 4:4–6; 1 John 2:15–17)

    B. The world is the enemy of God and the enemy of truth and righteousness. Satan is called the world's god, and friendship with it aligns one as God's enemy. (2 Corinthians 4:4; cf., James 4:4–6)

II. How the world pressures me to conform to its organized value system.

    A. It is the "extension" department for the appetites (1 John 2:16)

        1. The world offers its citizens what their fallen nature desires in attractive packages.

        2. Advertising, media presentations, and social programs offer fleshly appeal to attract attention and give the flesh what it wants.

    B. It is the "extension" department for the clever and deceptive lies of Satan and his kingdom. As the "god of this age," Satan introduces his deceptive rule over the nations. (2 Corinthians 4:4; Ephesians 2:1–2)

C. It pressures believers through its many organized and philosophic expressions to conform to its value system.

   1. Numerous world-organized structures pressure us to conform. The worlds of politics, education, finance, taxation, and religion are but a few.

   2. Philosophic and sensual appeal also pressures conformity. The worlds of entertainment, music, fashion, literature, and advertising add to the world's pressure to conform.

III. Resources that God has provided believers to overcome the pressures and temptations of the world system.

A. The truth embodied in the Gospel and the Christian faith equips believers to evaluate the world's fare. (1 John 5:1–5)

B. Knowledge of biblical ways to overcome the world's fleshly temptations will enable believers to resist the world's fleshly offerings. (Galatians 5:16–25)

C. Biblical knowledge of the believer's weapons of warfare against Satan's deceptive and threatening ways will equip believers to resist and overcome Satan's worldly tactics. (James 4:7–10)

REDEEMED MAN FACING
THE WORLD AND SATAN'S KINGDOM

I. Satan's kingdom: both external and internal.

A. External significance of the kingdom.

   1. Satan is called the god of this age or world (2 Corinthians 4:4). Satan's chief place of influence and rule is over the world. He and his wicked spirits work to control both the philosophy and organized structure of the world system.

   2. Though Satan is not omnipresent like God, he functions with a diverse, organized kingdom of spirit-beings who can communicate with him instantaneously from any geographic location in the world.

   3. Satan tries to force his evil plans and God-rejecting will upon nonbelievers by his control over them. (Ephesians 2:1–3)

   4. Satan tries to defeat believers by having his demonic

host directly attack them or use the world's organized structure to hinder them. (Ephesians 6:10–13)

B. Internal significance of the kingdom.

1. As personal, spirit-beings, Satan and his host of fallen angels are able to project thoughts, emotions, and a rebellious attitude into the mind, will, emotions, and body of a believer. With subtle, deceptive cleverness, internalized rule is attempted.

2. It is often difficult for believers to discern the difference between their own thoughts, emotions, and will from those of satanic origin. (Matthew 16:21–23)

3. If ground is given to the kingdom of darkness by a believer, internalized affliction, rule, and control will be experienced in that believer's life. (Ephesians 4:25–28; 2 Timothy 2:26)

II. An evil, supernatural kingdom.[4]

A. A kingdom ruled and headed by Satan.

1. One of, if not the most powerful of all of God's created beings. (Jude 9)

2. A created angelic being who rebelled against God and led one-third of the created angels to follow him in rebellion. (Revelation 12:4)

B. A kingdom organized and structured to defeat believers in their assigned task to evangelize the world and glorify God in the world. (Ephesians 6:10–12)

C. A powerful kingdom though infinitely inferior to God's which will ultimately be judged by consignment in the lake of fire. (Matthew 25:41; Revelation 20:10)

III. How Satan's kingdom tempts believers to do evil.

A. He tempts believers to deceive and to be deceived. (John 8:44; Acts 5:1–4)

B. He tempts believers to be fearful. (1 Peter 5:8–9)

C. He tempts believers to question God's Word, God's attributes, and God's will. (Genesis 3:1–6)

D. He accuses believers and attempts to torment them with false guilt. (Revelation 12:10–12)

E. He tempts us to destroy our lives or to take our lives by suicide. (Hebrews 2:14–15; John 8:43–45)

F. He tempts believers to excuse their fleshly sins in order to take advantage over them. (Ephesians 4:17–29)

G. He seeks to get us to justify our lack of forgiveness, to manipulate us into his control:

   1. Toward others. (Matthew 18:21–35)

   2. Toward self. (John 21:15–19; cf. Luke 22:31–37)

H. He tempts believers to pride. (1 Timothy 3:6–7)

   1. To use God's power for personal gain. (Luke 4:1–4)

   2. To worship Satan and to desire his power. (Luke 4:5–8)

   3. To test God's Word and His promises. (Luke 4:9–13)

IV. Resources for believers to defeat Satan and walk in freedom from Satan's rule.

A. God has provided four citadels that make a believer invincible over Satan's kingdom in the doing of God's will. (Ephesians 6:10–20)

   1. The believer's union with Jesus Christ in all of His person and work (Ephesians 6:10a). The phrase "Be strong in the Lord. . . . " or its equivalent is used more than forty times in Ephesians.

      a. In His name. (Acts 9:15; Colossians 3:17; Revelation 3:11–13)

      b. In His incarnation. (Colossians 1:22; 2:9–10)

      c. In His cross. (Galatians 2:20; Hebrews 2:14–15)

      d. In His resurrection. (Ephesians 2:6; John 14:19)

      e. In His ascension. (Ephesians 1:20–23; 2:6–7)

      f. In His glorification. (Ephesians 2:6; Romans 8:30)

      g. In His return. (Colossians 3:4; 1 Thessalonians 4:15–18)

   2. The person and work of the Holy Spirit (Ephesians 6:10b). We must keep the focus on His ministries to believers.

      a. Convicting ministry. (John 16:7–11)

      b. Indwelling ministry. (Romans 8:9)

      c. Sealing ministry. (Ephesians 1:13–14)

      d. Baptizing ministry. (1 Corinthians 12:13)

      e. Quickening ministry. (Romans 8:9–11)

      f. Interceding ministry. (Romans 8:26–27)

      g. Filling ministry.[5] (Ephesians 5:17–18)

3. The whole armor of God. (Ephesians 6:11–17)

      a. Belt of truth. (Ephesians 6:14a)

      b. Breastplate of righteousness. (Ephesians 6:14b)

      c. Shoes of peace. (Ephesians 6:15)

      d. Shield of faith. (Ephesians 6:16)

      e. Helmet of salvation. (Ephesians 6:17a)

      f. Sword of the spirit. (Ephesians 6:17b)

4. The allness of prayer. (Ephesians 6:18–20)

      a. The Paraclete of prayer (". . . in the Spirit").

      b. The persistence of prayer (". . . on all occasions").

      c. The parameters of prayer (". . . with all kinds of prayer").

      d. The protection of prayer (". . . be alert").

      e. The panorama of prayer (". . . for all the saints").

      f. The projection of prayer (". . . for me"). Paul wanted prepared, penetrating, courageous words to share.

B. To walk in freedom requires the aggressive application of the provided victory and not passive assumption. (Note frequent imperatives in Ephesians 6.)

PART THREE

RAISING LAMBS AMONG WOLVES

CHAPTER SEVEN

FREEDOM FOR PARENTS

W hen he was ten years old, Link saw his father's pornographic magazines. The magazines weren't hidden well, and Link began to look at the photographs inside. Later, as a single man in his late twenties he came to see me, to describe what he called "this bondage" that had developed.

The bondage involved sexual fantasies and accompanying masturbation. Link had read my book *The Adversary*, and regarded me, as the new pastor of his church, as a straw of hope. During our meeting he had begun a nervous litany of his deprecating view of himself when I interrupted.

"Link, are you a Christian believer?" He was a member of our church.

"Yes, I think I am, Pastor, but I wonder sometimes! I can't see how a Christian could still be doing the things I'm doing."

Link then gave a very clear testimony of his faith in the Lord Jesus Christ as his only hope for eternal life. Having been saved in a Billy Graham Crusade, Link told of how his new faith had brought him peace and an inward release from the guilt and self-hate that had plagued him all of his life. He'd been discipled by the friend who took him to the crusade. His baptism and membership in his church meant everything to him. Link never missed a meeting.

Tears coursed down Link's face as he recalled his conversion. "I'll never forget it. I started to pray with my counselor and as I asked Jesus to come into my life and cleanse all of my sins away something wonderful happened. I'd been weeping over my guilt and sinfulness but all of a sudden I realized my tears had changed. I was now crying out of sheer joy and gratitude. The weight of my sins lifted away and a sense of inner cleanness overwhelmed me.

"But that's why I feel so bad now. It was so great for several weeks, but when I began to slip back into some of my old sins again, everything began to change. I think I feel more guilt and defeat now than I did before I was saved."

Link's defeat concerned sensual, sexual sins. Seeing an attractive young lady on the street often triggered his sexual fantasy problem. Returning home, he would undress the woman in his mental fantasy and engage in sexual activity, which she welcomed and enjoyed in his imagination world of make-believe. After the accompanying masturbation was over, Link would hate himself. The guilt devastated him, but the defeat was like a shroud of death.

Link had diagnosed his own problem. "I must have a demon of lust controlling me. . . . I hate it so much, but I'm so helpless. I get drawn into it before I know what I'm doing. Will you help me get free from this wicked demon? Please!"

DEALING WITH OUR FLESH

Link is so typical of people with besetting sins that drive them and torment them with guilt. I use Link's story because his path to victory represents the biblical way God has provided us for freedom from sins that originate in fleshly desires and temptations.

Link's story shows how parents can influence their children to harm. Yet Link recognized that as an adult, he had to accept responsibility for his actions. We choose, often selfishly, to please our fleshly desires. And it starts very young. I remember our twin grandchildren, Cambria and Andrew, playing at our home during a visit when they were nine months old. Cambria was about three weeks ahead of Andrew in motor skills, and she would often hand him toys that she knew he liked.

As I watched this selfless display, I swelled with pride. *What a sweet picture of innocence*, I found myself thinking in my grandfatherly pride. Later, though, Andrew took something from Cambria, and I saw a different side to my granddaughter. She watched his labored struggle to stand to his feet; he swayed back and forth in his valiant effort to remain upright. At that moment Cambria reached over and gave him a little push on the shoulder. As Andrew tumbled into a twisted mass of arms and legs to the floor, my "perfection" image collapsed, too. She stood there looking so pleased with herself while Andrew whimpered his complaint.

Our fleshly nature appears in early childhood. Thus as adults, we Christian parents must learn how to handle our own flesh problems. We also must know how to teach our children biblical ways to deal with their flesh. Unless we experience our own spiritual victories we cannot model nor teach our children with confidence. Our "fleshly" sins range from anger and jealousy and self-advancement to more outward sexual sins. They keep us from a close relationship with God and confidence in leading our children. And, as we will see, much of it comes from our sinful nature.

What Is the Flesh?

Most evangelicals can accept the doctrine of the total depravity of man when we are talking theoretically. It's when we have to apply this doctrine to ourselves and to our children that we begin to draw back. Depravity doctrine recognizes that the corruption inherited from Adam's fall extends to every part of man's nature and all faculties of his being. This means there is nothing in man that can commend him or make him worthy in the presence of a holy, righteous God.[1]

Not every human being will exhibit his depravity with equal thoroughness, however. Some of the depraved will perform actions that appear good in human eyes. Nor will every depraved sinner indulge in all the forms of sin that he could. Yet, the sinful nature with its potential for sinful practices remains ingrained into the essential being of each person. It is an internal problem that is woven into the very nature of a person. David said our sinful nature not only began at birth, but it extended back even farther to the moment of conception. (See Psalm 51:5).The sin problem is deep indeed.

Theologians and Bible translators have struggled to find the proper words to describe this basic sin problem. The King James Version uses the word *flesh* to describe an internal struggle Christians face: "Walk in the Spirit, and ye shall not fulfil the lust of the flesh" (Galatians 5:16), KJV. Newer translations, such as the *New International Version*, use different words to convey this internal malady: "So I say, live by the Spirit, and you will not gratify the desires of the sinful nature."

"Lust of the flesh" and "desires of the sinful nature" both describe an internal problem with temptation to sin that all Christians face, including young children and teens. Our children need biblical insight (which parents can provide) to overcome this basic desire to live out a sinful life. We must not blame a Christian's temptation problems all on the Devil; that's an incomplete picture. At the core of the problem is an internal, depraved human condition, according to the Bible.

Understanding this basic doctrine is important to a believer's comprehension of the struggle he has with sin. A lifetime of biblical study and the counseling of many believers has convinced me that dealing with the flesh demands priority attention. Most believers don't know how to deal with this most basic human problem for every believer.

Our Sinful Nature

Our "fleshly" desires and temptations reflect the internal condition of our very person. We inherited this condition through the fall of Adam. Even after our new birth through saving faith, our fleshly desires remain totally wicked and depraved. These desires can never be reformed or improved because they derive from the sin of the Fall. Only by consistently applying the death and resurrection of Christ to our lives can we believers be free from the control of our fleshly desires.

The Lord Jesus Christ Himself gave the definitive statement about the nature of human defilement. He declared that defilement is an inward heart condition and not removed by outward ritual (such as the Pharisees washing their hands before eating). He told His inquiring disciples: "What comes out of a man is what makes him 'unclean.' For from within, out of men's hearts, come evil thoughts, sexual immorality, theft, murder, adultery, greed, malice, deceit, lewdness, envy, slander, arrogance and folly. All these evils come from inside and make a man 'unclean'" (Mark 7:20–23; cf. Matthew 15:18–20).

Our Lord Jesus Christ surely is speaking to this universal, depraved nature condition that all humanity inherited from the fall of Adam. It is this inner heart condition that reveals the defilement and potential for evil conduct and thoughts that required redeeming grace and saving forgiveness. No ceremonial washings or other outward religious practices could remedy this defilement.

The apostle Paul's descriptive list of the desires of the Christian's fleshly temptations closely parallels Jesus' list of activities revealing a defiled heart:

> The acts of the sinful nature [the flesh, NKJV] are obvious: sexual immorality, impurity and debauchery; idolatry and witchcraft; hatred, discord, jealousy, fits of rage, selfish ambitions, dissensions, factions and envy, drunkenness, orgies, and the like. (Galatians 5:19–21a)
>
> Put to death, therefore, whatever belongs to your earthly nature: sexual immorality, impurity, lust, evil desires and greed, which is idolatry. Because of these, the wrath of God is coming. You used to walk in these ways, in the life you once lived. But now you must rid yourselves of all such things as these: anger, rage, malice, slander, and filthy language from your lips. Do not lie to each other. . . . (Colossians 3:5–9a)

The Power to Overcome Temptations

These two listings are remarkably similar. The words of Jesus include all humanity. The words of Paul describe fleshly sins believers are to overcome. What does that tell us? A believer will face very similar temptations to those of nonbelievers. Because of their "flesh," Christians must deal with desires and temptations that are like those they faced before their new birth. The difference is that a believer does not need to be *ruled* and *controlled* by the temptations. His salvation has provided the Christian all he needs to "not fulfill the lust of the flesh" (Galatians 5:16b, NKJV). He can defeat those temptations.

I remember how freeing it was to Link when the Holy Spirit enabled him to understand this truth. Link thought the new birth would free him from the desires that had controlled him since his childhood. When the old desires began to tempt him after his conversion, overwhelming defeat and guilt resulted. It was false guilt. He was equating temptation's thoughts and desires with doing the sin. To Link they were equally sinful.

Satan, the accuser, used Link's ignorance of truth to lead him into sin: "You might as well go ahead and fantasize through this lust. You've already had the immoral thought. Now you need some action! Follow through! Since you're guilty anyway, enjoy the sin." A constant barrage of such mental accusations eventually broke through his resistance, and Link gave in to the temptation. Unbearable remorse and guilt followed.

Link had to recognize that temptation is not sin. He memorized Hebrews 4:14–15:

> Therefore, since we have a great high priest who has gone through the heavens, Jesus the Son of God, let us hold firmly to the faith we pronfess. For we do not have a high priest who is unable to sympathize with our weaknesses, but we have one who has been tempted in every way, just as we are—yet was without sin.

Even our Lord Jesus Christ felt the power of temptation. He knows the appeal it offers to a human being. As one of us, He experienced temptation but never sinned. He is now able and willing to help us walk in our freedom from the rule of our temptations and desires. Having provided our victory through His work, He now is able to shepherd us to enjoy it.

STEPS TO OVERCOME THE RULE OF YOUR FLESH

The fleshly desires are part of our lives as believers, but they need not control us. Here, in outline form, is what is required to overcome the rule of our flesh.

I. Know doctrinal truth upon which freedom is based: the three absolutes.

Colossians 3 is one of the classic New Testament passages that helps believers deal with their flesh. The chapter begins by focusing upon what I call three absolutes of grace. An absolute is a truth that stands alone. It is an indisputable fact because God Himself has made it true. Acting upon these three absolutes will enable us to walk in our freedom from fleshly rule.

A. Every believer has resurrection life. (Colossians 3:1–2)

This resurrection with Christ occurred even before we put our faith in Him as our personal Lord and Savior. It happened during the historic event itself. Christ's resurrection was your resurrection, according to the apostle Paul. The mighty power that raised the Lord Jesus Christ from the grave dwells in each believer's life. Our conduct is to flow out of understanding this truth. Since resurrection life dwells in us, we are to set our hearts and minds on heavenly things.

B. Every believer has union with Christ in His death. (Colossians 3:3)

At the cross, every believer died, even before he or she believed. The death of Christ was your death. It's your union with Christ that freed you from the penalty of sin and the power of sin to hold you in bondage. Our union with Christ as believers is so secure and safe: "Your life is now hidden with Christ in God." Understanding this lofty doctrinal truth is crucial to overcoming the desires of our flesh.

C. Every believer has union with Christ in His second coming. (Colossians 3:4)

This absolute hasn't happened yet, but it is just as certain as the first two that are based on historic events. Every believer will appear with Christ in the glory of His second coming. Absolutes are like that. Since they are based upon God's person, what is yet to happen is just as sure as what has already happened.

II. Know the necessary biblical steps in order to apply your freedom.

Great doctrinal truth based on the absolutes of God is not meant to be passively accepted. These truths are to be lived in the crucible of daily life. Note how clear this is made in this matter of walking in our freedom from the rule of our fleshly desires and temptations.

A. Walk in honest admission and confession. (Colossians 3:5–10)

The word *therefore* in verse 5 ("Put to death, therefore . . .") points us back to the three absolutes of grace mentioned in the first four verses and the first point of this outline. Believers can walk in freedom from the rule of this long list of sins when we apply these three absolutes.

According to Galatians 5:19, "the acts of the sinful nature are obvious." To whom are these acts of the flesh obvious? They are obvious to God and to our Lord Jesus Christ. God knows these desires flow to us from our fallen condition, and He wants us to know it, too. Understanding this truth is crucial to freedom. We must not expect more of ourselves than what God has presently provided us. This truth can liberate us from much false guilt.

B. Walk in the truth of your death with Christ.

Four key New Testament texts declare the believer's death with Christ or command that we act as those who are dead to our sinful nature: Romans 6:11; Galatians 5:24; Colossians 3:3; 3:5. Each text speaks to the necessity of recognizing how God has equipped the believer to overcome the desires of the flesh by the cross of Christ.

C. Walk in the control of the Holy Spirit. (Galatians 5:16, 18, 22–23, 25)

When the Holy Spirit controls the believer a much different life is produced than what the fleshly, earthly nature can produce. We need to remember our identity as Christ's followers. According to Colossians 3:12, we are God's chosen people, holy, and dearly loved.

God chose us to be the channels through which His message of love and grace would flow to the world. God calls us holy, even though we may not feel at times we are living in a holy way. Justification has made every believer holy in God's sight. The very righteousness of Jesus Christ has been credited to each believer in his standing before God. And though we may struggle with earthly, fleshly sins (as the Colossae believers were to whom Paul was writing) we are greatly loved. The Lord is on your side. He is not angry and displeased with you because of your failures. He loves you.

According to Colossians 3:12, you are to "clothe yourselves with compassion, kindness, humility, gentleness and patience." Ask yourself: "Who was compassionate, kind, humble, gentle, and patient?" Jesus! Be like Jesus, is the imperative. You *can be* more and more like Jesus. As we allow the power that raised Jesus Christ from the dead to control our minds, wills, emotions, and bodies, Christ's likeness will be seen in each of us. This is the Holy Spirit's work. He is the one who brings resurrection life into the experience of each believer.

PRAYERS IN APPLYING THE STEPS

The three steps under point II above are practical and can be applied through prayer and by following Christ. Let's consider each step in practical terms.

First, *honest admission and confession* of temptation clearly requires that we be honest with ourselves and the Lord. When a fleshly temptation or desire first presents itself to our consciousness, we are to be honest in addressing our need to our Lord, praying about it specifically. We should state it to Him in a manner such as this:

*Lord Jesus Christ, my old fleshly nature is tempting me to
_____ (name the temptation, e.g., lust, anger, gossip) and I
know that if it's left to itself, it is wicked enough to cause me to sin
against You.*

Such honesty is liberating in itself. It helps you recognize
your need. You don't need to "save face" by trying to convince
yourself that your flesh isn't as bad as God states it to be. Honest
admission is a part of recognizing our need to avail ourselves of
the absolutes of grace.

Second, acting upon the truth that *we have died with
Christ* and so should "count [ourselves] dead to sin but alive to
God in Christ Jesus" (Romans 6:11), requires we acknowledge
this truth to Christ in prayer. You may want to express your
freedom to overcome sin this way:

*Lord Jesus Christ, I affirm that through the work of Your cross I am
dead with You to the rule and control of my flesh and its desire to
_____ (name of fleshly temptation being experienced at that
moment, i.e., anger, lust, etc.).*

Being free from sin's control does not mean our Lord
promised that we would be free from experiencing the temptations of our flesh. Just the opposite is true. He told us these are
the temptations and desires our flesh will present to us as we
live our earthly lives. It's only after we go to be with our Lord
that the temptations are forever gone. I believe this to be a
major reason why the Lord planned that each of us would be
left to deal with our fleshly desires: Dealing with them keeps us
close to the Cross and the work done for us there.

Third, to *walk in the control of the Holy Spirit,* we must
turn to the Holy Spirit. The Holy Spirit doesn't force His control upon us. God respects our dignity too much for that. He
waits for us to ask the Holy Spirit to do what He is within us to
do. In prayer, we should take this third step in this manner:

*Blessed Holy Spirit, I ask You now to replace this fleshly desire
that is tempting me to be _____ (state the fleshly appeal; i.e.,*

anger, lust, jealousy, etc.) with the fruit of Your control. Put within my mind, will, emotions, and body Your love, joy, peace, patience, and all the virtues that my Lord Jesus Christ enables me to live out for His glory.

Of course, as Ephesians 5:18 notes, we are to continue being filled with the Spirit. Each fleshly desire needs this application of truth every time we feel its pressure. All three steps should be applied moment by moment as we walk through each day.

These three steps are simple but profound. Some have mistakenly thought that if they have a special filling or baptism of the Holy Spirit they will then be able to overcome their flesh. Not so! That may bless our witnessing ministry, but that is not the way to freedom from the rule of your flesh. These three steps will enable each believer to employ his freedom as the flesh tempts with its desires.

USING THE BIBLICAL PRESCRIPTION

After our second meeting together, Link could repeat these three steps back to me with accuracy and confidence. I felt he was ready to go out and meet his temptation. By using his new biblical knowledge, he would do well in overcoming his lustful perversion, I thought. I was in for a disappointment.

A few days later, Link called me on the phone. In great desperation he wept out his distress: "Oh, Pastor Bubeck! You must help me get rid of this demon of lust. I just failed again and I'm so ashamed—"

"Link, what are the three biblical steps to overcoming your flesh?" I interrupted his lament by forcing him to consider where he lost the battle. There was total silence on the other end of the phone. I waited.

"I can't remember," Link confessed. "This demon of lust has me too upset at the moment."

"Link," I responded, "I don't have anything more to share with you if you won't use the biblical way to victory that the Lord has provided."

He apologized for not remembering, and I patiently taught the three steps again. Having learned them earlier, he found they came back quickly. Then I gave him some tough love therapy: "Link, don't bother to call me again or ask for any appointment if you can't give these steps to me. I won't talk to you or see you until you can satisfy me that you are using this biblical prescription."

After prayer, we concluded the call. Link was in church on Sunday, but he didn't greet me at the door. He was in the mid-week prayer service, but again we had no conversation. I wondered if I'd been too tough on him. I was dying to know how he was doing. Several more days passed before he finally called.

On hearing his voice on the phone, I asked, "Link, what are the three biblical steps God has given us to overcome our flesh?"

His response was quick and decisive: "Walk of honesty! Walk of death! And walk in the Spirit!"

I felt ecstatic! After I congratulated him, he responded, "That really works, doesn't it?"

It works because it is the applying of biblical truth. Link did need to deal with a demonic problem, but I knew that if he didn't learn how to deal with his flesh, he would make no progress against the kingdom of darkness. We'll deal with that problem in the next chapter.

Through my years of ministry, I have tried to teach the practical steps to fleshly victory to all to whom I've been privileged to minister. Despite my best efforts from the pulpit, I've later had to recognize that many, like Link, were not able to bring the teaching into practice when it was most needed. Counseling opportunities showed me that many could not give these steps back to me. Some were able, however, and often responded with joy. It really does work because it's using God's truth to insure one's freedom. I've determined that through patient repetition, I will just go on sharing this simple plan. We must live it out and we must share it with those believers we disciple.

TEACHING OUR CHILDREN
THE BIBLICAL PRINCIPLES

Link learned how to deal with his first-line enemy as an adult. How much better when we prepare our children while young to deal with their first-line enemy. Instead, well-meaning Christian parents often fall into a dangerous trap of trying to help their children reform or improve their fleshly desires. By discipline and shame tactics, we try to force our children to live out better behavior. Even after our children come to know the Lord Jesus Christ as personal Lord and Savior, we use these tactics.

Anger, jealousy, quarreling, and factions are common fleshly sins all children experience. If they know the Lord Jesus, we should be teaching them about their spiritual resources. Yes, discipline does have its place. Children need to learn that these sins are unacceptable and wrong. They are not only wrong because they create miserable family living, but they are wrong in God's sight. However, discipline doesn't change and free a child from sinful behavior. Shame fails even more tragically. Shame creates guilt feelings and a loss of self-worth. "I'm no good" thoughts and feelings begin to rule a child who is shamed and put down for his bad behavior.

Wise parents, however, will *begin to train children in the biblical principles of defeating sinful nature temptations*. You can introduce your children to these principles at a very young age. It will require patience, persistence, and repeated times of loving instruction, but the rewards will be phenomenal.

Remember Suzy in chapter 2? This five-year-old experienced out-of-control rages caused by a generational transfer problem. Her aging grandfather had lived out a lifetime of cruel, drunken rages, often abusing his son, Jim. Only as Jim and his wife practiced protective warfare prayer over their daughter was the demonic control eliminated from Suzy's life.

However, her tendency toward quick anger was a temperament and sinful nature problem that demonic powers did not create. Suzy was a Christian. She'd received the Lord Jesus Christ when she was four. After Suzy's parents had broken the demonic activity, they began to patiently teach her how to break the fleshly nature rule of anger. It amazed them and me to see Suzy quickly understand. Her keen mind and spiritual sensitivity helped a five-year-old deal with her anger problem.

She understood well the biblical principles of being dead with Christ and controlled by the Spirit. Her mother would hear her say, "I'm dead with Jesus to the control of anger. I ask the Holy Spirit to put love and joy and peace inside my heart." Suzy's behavior took a radical change. Her anger came under control.

Suzy is now ten years of age. It has taken patient teaching and much repetition by her godly parents, but Suzy is learning to consistently walk in her freedom. What discipline and reasoning couldn't do, grace and truth are doing.

GUIDELINES FOR TEACHING
VICTORY OVER THE FLESH TO CHILDREN

Teaching your child the biblical principles of this chapter are vital. If your child knows Jesus as his or her Savior, it is not too early to start. Here are several guidelines to remember as you work with your child to teach the three steps to freedom from fleshly rule.

1. Be sure that you as a Christian parent understand and practice your own freedom from fleshly rule.

2. Make sure that your child has made a personal decision of asking the Lord Jesus Christ into his/her life as Lord and Savior.

3. Watch for the major "besetting" sin evident in each child's life. (Anger, lying, greed, and jealousy are common to children.) Arrange a quiet talk time about the problem and teach the three steps to freedom on the child's level of understanding.

4. Pray for the Lord to help the child apply his freedom.

5. Be prepared for repetition and further application of this truth as the child grows and other fleshly nature sins appear.

6. When you note the successful use of the steps to overcome the flesh, commend the child and let him/her know that you noticed.

7. Carefully avoid dependence on shame and discipline to transform the fleshly nature. Depend on the application of spiritual truth to effect change.

8. Watch for evidences that might indicate demonic attempts to rule your child. Consistently practice aggressive spiritual warfare protection of your children.

PREVENTING DEMONIC HARASSMENT

Raising healthy lambs among wolves requires that the shepherds stay strong—confident and able to ward off the attacks their sheep may face. That means parents must themselves know not only what to do for their children, but stay strong themselves. We saw in the previous chapter how to strengthen ourselves and our children against fleshly attacks. Now we must consider what happens if we let sin progress in the lives of ourselves or our children—the lambs we want to protect.

Continuing to indulge in sin can open us and our family to demonic harassment. In Link's case, that is what happened. He returned to my office in frustration after having had some victories, but feeling equally strong temptations afterward.

"Pastor, I don't want to be disrespectful of your efforts to help me," he said during our meeting, "but I still think I have a demon of lust that is trying to rule and torment me. I'm using my victory over my flesh on a regular basis now. It has wonderfully helped me, but sometimes I seem to hear voices in my mind that laugh at me. Then, the temptation starts all over again, and I wonder about my sanity."

Link's query was obviously sincere. He was still hurting in his struggle. I was not surprised. His mention of his father's being into pornography opened the door to the possibility of a generational transfer problem. The other red flag suggesting demonic harassment related to the lengthy period that Link had willingly practiced his fleshly sin of perverted sexual lust. He would need to deal with the realm of unclean spirits before his freedom would be complete.

Experience and biblical common sense had taught me that you don't make progress against the kingdom of darkness if fleshly sin is being practiced. Ephesians 4 proved to be very eye-opening to Link. He came to understand that excusing fleshly sins always leads on to deeper problems with sin.

NO EXCUSES FOR SINS OF THE FLESH

As parents, we must respond promptly to sins we observe in ourselves—and in our children. If we love them, we want to help them from sliding into deeper problems, including demonic harassment. To do this, we will face—or help our children face—their own fleshly attitudes or actions. The Scriptures warn us against excusing sin in our lives. Consider the warnings about treating fleshly sins with indifference in Ephesians 4:17–32, a passage Link and I looked at carefully.

In verses 17–18, the apostle Paul warns the Christians:

> So I tell you this, and insist on it in the Lord, that you must no longer live as the Gentiles do, in the futility of their thinking. They are darkened in their understanding and separated from the life of God because of the ignorance that is in them due to the hardening of their hearts.

The words *insist* and *must* convey the urgency of the message to follow. Believers are not to live like Gentiles or nonbelievers in this context. Unbelievers suffer from a futile thought process that is "darkened" in understanding the truth.

This darkness probably conveys the truth of Ephesians 2:1–3 that the prince of darkness controls them as "the ruler of the kingdom of the air, the spirit who is now at work in those who are disobedient." Non-Christians are ruled by both the appetites of their flesh and the subtle rule of Satan's kingdom. They do not realize this, but so states the Word of God.

Paul next explained the principle of increased bondage: "Having lost all sensitivity, they have given themselves over to sensuality so as to indulge in every kind of impurity, with a continual lust for more" (v. 19). The practice of fleshly sins always leads into more and more bondage. "That's certainly the way it is with me," Link confessed. "Except I am very sensitive to the sensual desires that control me."

Fleshly sins inevitably get worse. It's like an addiction: The more you try it, the more you want to repeat it. As you continue, you typically want a little more for your excitement or "high." It matters little whether one is a believer or a nonbeliever. The more one indulges the appetites of the flesh, the more deeply his desire for more of the same leads into other sins.

Indulging the desires of the "old self" has no place in a Christian's life, according to Paul: "Surely you heard of him and were taught in him in accordance with the truth that is in Jesus. You were taught, with regard to your former way of life, to put off your old self, which is being corrupted by its deceitful desires" (vv. 21–22).

The truth that is in Jesus should instruct our lives. Following His teaching and the Holy Spirit's guidance will lead to the putting off of the rule and control of fleshly desires. Freedom does not come simply because one has been saved. Teaching and an active "putting off" are necessary on the part of the reborn one. How is this done?

I believe the putting off takes place as one follows the first two steps to victory over the flesh as taught in the previous chapter. Putting off the desires of the old self requires (1) an honest confession and (2) recognizing we are "dead with Christ" to sin. We must acknowledge quickly our fleshly desire, realizing its potential to lead us into sin. A simple prayer could be, "Lord Jesus, my fleshly nature is at it again, and I know that it's wicked enough to lead me into sin if left to itself." Then we must recognize our need to die to sin; that is how we "put off" the desires of the "old self." A simple prayer could be, "Lord Jesus, I affirm that because of Your sacrificial death on the Cross, I am dead to the rule and control of this fleshly desire."

The victory requires a third step, to have a renewed mind. Paul wrote, ". . . be made new in the attitude of your minds; and . . . put on the new self, created to be like God in true righteousness and holiness" (Ephesians 4:23–24).

How does a believer do this? By reaching out at the moment of temptation and asking the Holy Spirit to do what He is within your person to do. That's having the Holy Spirit control your attitudes (step three mentioned in the previous chapter). A sample prayer (like the one Link said) would be: "I now ask the Holy Spirit to supplant and replace this fleshly desire I am experiencing with the fruit of His control. Put within me Your love, joy, peace, patience, and all that I need to respond to this temptation as my Savior would."

As a believer practices these simple doctrinal applications of truth, freedom begins to come from the rule of the flesh. Link's problem, however, did not fully abate as he employed these doctrinal truths to his sexual defeats. Paul tells us why in verses 25–27: "Therefore, each of you must put off falsehood and speak truthfully to his neighbor, for we are all members of one body. 'In your anger do not sin': Do not let the sun go down while you are still angry, and do not give the devil a foothold."

Both lying and anger are expressions of the desires of the fleshly nature. (See Colossians 3:9 and Galatians 5:19–21.) Lying must be overcome in the believer's life. Anger must not be held onto and justified when it originates in our flesh. We must not excuse it with faulty words. "I have good reason to be angry. Did you see what that person did to me?" Link had to deal with his lust; others deal with their anger. Many of us deal with either the temptations to deceive or to show anger; sometimes both temptations plague us. We must not excuse these as "lesser sins" or "just part of who I am."

When we fail to deal with each sin as it shows itself, when we do not apply our victory in a biblical way, we give the Devil a "foothold" (v. 27). Footholds inevitably become strongholds to facilitate the rule of the powers of darkness. An unclean spirit uses the "foothold" as a point of rule and control in the area of the ground given. Link's problem had become more than fleshly rule; the laughter he heard in his mind as he applied his victory over his flesh gave evidence of such a stronghold. There were other evidences too, but we must not fear even this dark possibility. It does tell us of how serious the matter is of practicing fleshly sin.

RESISTING THE SPIRITS

Unresolved sin problems of the flesh open the door for footholds of unique satanic control of any child's or adult's life. But even then, once the believer begins to deal with his fleshly sin according to biblical guidelines, Satan's footholds or strongholds will crumble. This was Link's experience, and it can be your experience—or your child's. I took time to carefully teach Link about the authority that he had over Satan through his union with Christ. When voices, tauntings, cursings, or other demonic harassments were confusing his mind, Link learned to apply his resistance authority in a biblical way. Freedom soon came into his tormented life.

His resistance prayer is shown below as a model you or your child can use when chronic sin indicates a possible satanic stronghold.

In the name of my Lord Jesus Christ and by the power of His blood I come against the wicked spirit of _____ (name symptom of assault) and all of his hosts. I command you to cease your wicked work against me and you and your hosts must leave me and go where my Lord Jesus Christ sends you. I ask the Holy Spirit to search out all control points of my person and evict these dark powers from my presence. I yield my whole person only to the rule and control of my Lord Jesus Christ. I ask the Holy Spirit to sanctify and fully control those areas of my person where the powers of darkness have done their intrusive work.

A resistance application of this kind must not be thought of as a magical incantation or formula. It is only the truth applied that sets one free from the rule of darkness. Understanding of the truth and its sincere, consistent application are what brings the believer—man, woman, or child—to freedom.

Interestingly, the actions of wicked spirits can be compared to those of spoiled children. Parents have the biblical right to expect and receive obedient actions and responses from their children. The parent's superior strength adds the ability, and parents are to firmly insist on proper behavior. However, obedience does not happen in all situations, especially when you have a strong-willed child. Only with persuasive patience and firm discipline will most children respectfully obey.

Wicked spirits are likewise strong-willed. They have assignments from their superiors in the kingdom of darkness. They are out to "steal and kill and destroy," according to Jesus (John 10:10a). Their task is to rob you of all that the Lord has purchased for you in victorious service. Each is determined to fulfill his assignment, though all know fully your authority over them because of your union with the person and work of Christ. *They don't want you to know that.* They will not usually obey you when you first use your authority. They will use every available deception and trick to convince you that they are not going to relinquish control.

This is why patient, persistent application of truth is necessary in spiritual warfare. Link followed through by consistently using both his victory over his flesh and the resistance of unclean spirits. A long-time walk of defeat began to turn around. It was not a quick fix, however. The generational transfer issue needed to be renounced and the consistent living out of his freedom had to be applied. Once the kingdom of darkness has its hooks of control into one's life, the return to a walk of freedom will be ruthlessly opposed by those evil powers. That's the way of God's plan for the believer's growth in grace. When Link saw God's plan, he was able to enter into it with contentment and faithful practice.

BEWARE OF THE KINGDOM OF DARKNESS

Protecting parents need to be free parents. Control and oppressive dictation from evil wolves of darkness in a parent's life will weaken their child's protection. If parental freedom is not established or reclaimed, an open door of opportunity exists for wolves to focus attack on the parent's offspring. That conclusion seems implicit from our discussion of the generational transfer problem in chapter 3. (See again Exodus 34:7 and Deuteronomy 5:9.)

An important foundation for gaining or maintaining personal freedom from the rule of evil wolves is to have a biblical understanding of our battle with darkness. Just what and who is involved in the believer's wrestling with supernatural evil? What can help me stand free in my own experience so that I can effectively help my child? We devote the remaining pages of this chapter to recognizing the nature of the opposition we face. A healthy respect and clear understanding of the kingdom of darkness are essential for you and your children to find spiritual freedom.

Here are three key reminders about the kingdom of darkness, which is ruled by Satan. These reminders are cautions as well, for they show us the adversary has great power and a diabolical purpose. Fortunately, our resources as Christians are greater than Satan's. As the apostle John assured us, "the one who is in you [Jesus] is greater than the one who is in the world" (1 John 4:4).

A STRUCTURED KINGDOM UNDER CHRIST

First, the kingdom of darkness is an organized structure of supernatural evil, part of Christ's creation and subservient to Him. The Bible clearly teaches that the Lord Jesus Christ created the kingdom and all others, and as the creator He oversees it and its inhabitants.

He is the image of the invisible God, the firstborn over all creation. For by him all things were created: things in heaven and on earth, visible and invisible, whether thrones or powers or rulers or authorities; all things were created by him and for him. He is before all things, and in him all things hold together. (Colossians 1:15–17)

As a structured kingdom, this throne of darkness still is subservient to Christ. Thus, in Christ's power, we can stand against the Devil's schemes:

> Put on the full armor of God so that you can take your stand against the devil's schemes. For our struggle is not against flesh and blood, but against the rulers, against the authorities, against the powers of this darkness of this dark world and against the spiritual forces of evil in the heavenly realms. (Ephesians 6:11–12)

Satan is not a creator. The Colossians text makes this very clear. Having been created by the Lord Jesus Christ, the thrones and powers ("dominions," NKJV) where Satan and his demons roam still are under the full authority of Jesus. Indeed, Jesus has won the final victory over Satan and all the fallen angels. They cannot even "consist" (Colossians 1:17, NKJV) and hold together apart from the sustaining power of the Creator. For sovereign purposes known only to God the kingdom of darkness is allowed to continue to rebel and function until God's perfect time to judge Satan and his host. At that moment, God will cast all the fallen spirit beings into the lake of fire prepared for them. (See Matthew 25:41; Revelation 20:10.)

An Inferior Kingdom with a Counterfeit Plan

Second, Satan's kingdom has a counterfeit, parallel plan for nearly everything God does in His perfect plan of redemption. Though Satan has only temporary influence, he has a counterfeit plan—a crafty imitation of the real. We must not forget that Satan is exceedingly clever. When he fell in his rebellion, Satan did not lose the gifts and genius that God put into him. He is a master deceiver. When talking of Satan, many adjectives are required: *powerful, beautiful, clever, crafty, subtle, deceptive, mighty, ruthless,* and *sinister* are a few. He also is *enslaving, manipulating, cruel, brutal, angry, mean,* and *destroying,* as is his kingdom.

Here are five ways his dark kingdom counterfeits, or false-
ly imitates, everything God has done:

1. Satan offers those who follow him a counterfeit family
   (cf. Matthew 13:36–43). In explaining the parable of the
   sower (Matthew 13:24–30), the Lord Jesus illustrated
   how clever Satan is to intermingle his family members
   with the Lord's family (vv. 37–43), comparing them to
   weeds growing among the wheat. Those following Satan
   will be so plentiful and deceptive that they will even min-
   gle in our churches and be hard to detect. Like family, they
   will find much in common as they seek pleasure, independence, and their own approaches to life, apart from God.

2. Satan has created a counterfeit gospel (Galatians 1:6–9;
   1 Timothy 4:1–3). Satan has his own "good news" which
   he uses to pervert the ways of truth and enslave the
   nondiscerning. This "gospel" is one of greed, legalism,
   and twisted perversions concerning foods and even
   marriage, according to the apostle Paul. In our day, the
   extreme of this "gospel" has appeared in published
   form as the so-called *Satanic Bible*. New Age teaching,
   the prosperity gospel, Hinduism, Buddhism, and neo-
   Christian cults like Mormonism, Jehovah's Witnesses,
   and Christian Science must be placed with Satan's
   gospel. There are many shapes and shades to the counterfeit gospel Satan uses to pervert and confuse the
   message of the Gospel of Jesus Christ.

3. Satan also has established counterfeit ministers (2 Corinthians 10–11). A counterfeit gospel must be relayed by
   counterfeit messengers. The apostle Paul warns of those
   who pose as ministers of God and His gospel but in reality are ministers of the Devil. Their goal is to exalt Satan's
   realm and destroy the kingdom of God. Paul climaxed
   his warning with these forceful words about their end
   danger: "his ministers also transform themselves into
   ministers of righteousness, whose end will be according
   to their works" (2 Corinthians 11:15, NKJV; cf. vv. 13–14).

4. Satan offers a counterfeit righteousness (Romans 9–10). Man's most serious problem arises when he goes about to invent his own righteous standards while passing up the righteousness of God. Such deception has its origin in the master deceiver, Satan himself. He continues to mislead people to believe that their own actions done in their own way can please God. In Romans 9 and 10, Paul details the false righteousness that people embrace in lieu of God's true righteousness. A key verse is Romans 10:3: "For they being ignorant of God's righteousness, and seeking to establish their own righteousness, have not submitted to the righteousness of God" (NKJV).

5. Satan seeks his own, counterfeit worship (1 Corinthians 11:14–33). Satan's desire to exalt himself to be as God includes his desire to receive worship just as God receives worship from those who love Him. It's still surprising to me the number of people who have been tempted to worship the Devil. Yet they are in good company, for Jesus Himself was tempted to worship Satan (Matthew 4:9b). The Lord Jesus surely understands that temptation because it also came to Him there in the wilderness. We must resist such temptation. The answer Jesus gave is still the best: "Away from me, Satan! For it is written, 'Worship the Lord your God, and serve him only'" (Matthew 4:10).

A Kingdom Ruled by Deception

Third, Satan rules his kingdom by deception, fear, and ignorance. Satan has no reality to present. Everything about him is counterfeit, deceptive, and misleading. Even when he tells the truth, he twists it into a lie. He quoted the truth of Scripture in his temptations of the Lord Jesus, but his purpose in doing so was to tempt and deceive. This is still his chief tactic against God's people. Jesus understood that ignorance of the truth can enslave, while knowledge of the truth sets free. So He told His followers:

If you abide in My word, you are My disciples indeed. And you shall know the truth, and the truth shall make you free. . . . Therefore, if the Son makes you free, you shall be free indeed." (John 8:31–32, 36, NKJV)

Jesus also knew that those who follow Satan are often deluded and unable to comprehend spiritual things. Thus Jesus said to the deluded religious leaders of His day:

Why do you not understand My speech? Because you are not able to listen to My word. You are of your father the devil, and the desires of your father you want to do. He was a murderer from the beginning, and does not stand in the truth, because there is no truth in him. When he speaks a lie, he speaks from his own resources, for he is a liar and the father of it. (John 8:43–44, NKJV.)

Deception and its fear can only succeed when we are ignorant of the truth. Satan can and does hold his bondage on a believer and his family when they function within the sphere of the Devil's deceptive tactics. Ignorance concerning truth is as useful to Satan's purposes as the believing of his blatant lies. This is why good Bible teaching and doctrinal study are so necessary to walk in personal freedom. To protect our children from the rule of darkness in their lives, parents must know the truth of their authority to apply the truth of God to their children's needs.

Satan is an illusionist. He deceives by offering us a pretend life that is not real. He uses the world and its media methods as his theater to spread his illusions. Televisions, videos, movies, and the world's music offer a menu of pretend. They offer a false message about what constitutes the "good life." Revenge is presented as a desirable virtue. Enjoying the sensual and finding sexual conquest are touted as bringing ultimate pleasure. Movies and TV shows portray those with money or power as achieving maximum success. These entertainment media depict the mysteries of occult power as exciting and worthy of pursuit.

Satan's kingdom is behind this deceptive offering of perverted values. Only godly, Christian parents stand between their children and Satan's plans for his deceptive control.

OUR SPIRITUAL RIGHTS AS PARENTS

As believers and parents, our understanding of these truths can give us confidence and direction as we rear children. Lance and Betty Faith are perfect examples. Spiritually mature believers, they served several years as missionaries with an evangelical missionary agency; today Lance is an elder in his local church. It was my privilege to have a part in discipling them in the application of their victory over the world, the flesh, and the Devil. They became faithful warriors who learned how to fight a good fight.

Yet despite their faithful efforts, their son, Max, became a spiritual rebel. Lance and Betty blamed much of their son's problems on their lives before they became Christians. Having been saved later in life, they were aware that Max had suffered from the fallout of their own sinful rebellions. They feared that he had absorbed some of their stubborn, rebellious example as a young boy.

Lance and Betty kept praying and solicited the prayers of their Christian friends in behalf of Max. Little progress seemed evident. Max sought to prove his independence by living a sinful lifestyle. The result was a fractured personal life and a fractured relationship between Max and his parents that lasted for seven long years.

"It was a lonely, painful time," confessed Lance. "It was like a desert where our expectations were low and our hope was almost lost."

God was at work, however, in the most important place. Lance began to review his own responsibility before the throne of grace. God's Word became very personal to him. Learning about his generational tie to his son brought new insight to Lance. And soon an intense review of Satan's limits and the Scripture's truths accomplished a breakthrough. First, though, his study of Hebrews 7:1–10 opened Lance's eyes to a new concept. Four verses, 5 and 8–10, stood out.

Now the law requires the descendants of Levi who become priests to collect a tenth from the people—that is, their broth-

ers—even though their brothers are descended from Abraham.
. . . In the one case, the tenth is collected by men who die; but in
the other case, by him who is declared to be living. One might
even say that Levi, who collects the tenth, paid the tenth
through Abraham, because when Melchizedek met Abraham,
Levi was still in the body of his ancestor.

Though this text emphasizes the superiority of the
Melchizedek priesthood over the Aaronic priesthood, Lance
recognized something else. The whole line of reasoning was
based on two statements: The reference to "descended from
Abraham" and the reference to Levi being "still in the body of
his ancestor" when Abraham paid tithes to Melchizedek spoke
deeply to Lance. He saw in a new way how close his own tie
was to Max.

What happened after this eye-opening passage spoke to
Lance is a fitting climax to this chapter. For the encouragement
of readers who may have a burden for a wayward son or daughter, let me quote from Lance and Betty's written account, which
they have allowed to be published here.

"I reviewed spiritual warfare concerning Satan's holds or
rights to my son. It slowly came to me that I, too, had rights in
my son's life. I [began] to investigate them. I discovered that as
his father, I had the following rights:

1. Through Moses, my Lord Jesus Christ comanded me to
   train my son to walk according to the Scripture. (Deuteronomy 4:9)

2. Through the apostle Paul, Jesus instructed me to train
   and admonish my son according to the Scriptures.
   (Ephesians 6:4)

3. Through Solomon, the Lord Jesus Christ admonished
   me to rear my son in dedication to the Lord. I must
   teach him how to live his life so that it would please the
   Lord. I was responsible to motivate my son to want to
   carry out all of the Lord's Word in his spiritual life.
   (Proverbs 22:6; 29:17, etc.)

4. Through Paul and by His example, the Lord

Jesus instructed me to love Max unconditionally and continually. (1 Corinthians 13:4–13)

"Seeing these precepts triggered deeper spiritual awareness. I saw that Satan had gained ground or rights to rule in my son's soul over his emotions, intellect, and will. His sinful lifestyle and rebellion granted those rights. But I also saw that I as his father had a bond and spiritual priesthood in Max's life that had been established by Jesus Christ. I knew that it was up to Betty and me to carry out these God-given rights to help our son to freedom. As ambassadors of Jesus Christ, we could enter the battle in our son's behalf to help regain the lost territory."

And so Lance shut himself away with the Lord in intensive prayer. There he spoke out against the realm of wicked spirits that had direct or indirect rights to rule over his son.

"As a Christian believer and as Max's father, I commanded them to hear me without responding by any overt activity. I reviewed against them my rights as expressed in the above four points. I affirmed strongly that Max, as the fruit of his mother's womb and my loins, was only given to Jesus Christ, our Lord and Savior. I then confessed all known sin of my son to my heavenly Father as Job and Nehemiah had done (Job 1:5; Nehemiah 1:6), asking the Lord to claim back all the ground given through the merit of His blood."

Lance's prayer was powerful and confident:

In the name of my Lord Jesus Christ, I bind the evil powers assigned to rule Max from the full use of their power over Max. By faith, I affirm that I have planted Jehovah Nissi's banner in the center of my son's soul. I command that all demons assigned to rule and destroy Max must daily see that banner of Jehovah's ownership over his life.

Then Max's father prayed that God would cover his son with the person of the Holy Spirit "like a blanket assigned to bring him back to the reality of God's truth."

Lance "was particularly concerned that Max would know what God expected of him and would be aware that God's wrath is very real," he wrote. His description continues:

"Daily we entered into this kind of prayer battle. Betty and I prayed along the list outlined above, expecting the Holy Spirit to apply His perfect doctrinal understanding as He brought our prayers to the Father. We affirmed that we were praying in the will of our Savior in accord to our responsibility to our son (1 John 5:14–15).

"Compared to the seven years we had waited, within a short passage of time, our son's life began to change. At first it was a glimmer of hope but it grew to a complete reversal of his rebellious, indifferent spiritual attitudes and ways. The light of the Lord slowly rekindled. His eyes returned to a sparkle of love from a glare of defiance and challenge."

The Faiths conclude their written account with a wonderful outcome: "Our son is now walking with Jesus as his Lord. He exhibits significant signs of Christlike growth. As my wife and I took our doctrinal stand on God's Word and poured out continuous, unconditional love upon our son, God honored our total, unexplainable faith. We were convinced that Christ's defeat of the powers of darkness in our son's life was total. We saw and are still seeing it happen. Jesus Christ was and is victorious!"

SPIRITISTIC ACTIVITY IN CHILDREN

Todd seemed to be a resourceful child and quite capable of creative invention in his patterns of play. In fact he became so creative that he enjoyed playing by himself more than playing with his siblings or friends. When he played by himself, his mother often heard him carrying on a conversation with an imaginary friend who played with him. His mother attributed his talking to his creative imagination and gift for fantasy. She saw no hint of danger until one day she overheard him talking in a conversational tone that seemed to indicate that Todd was actually hearing verbal responses in his conversation with his imaginary playmate.

Todd's mother later confessed her troubled concern but did not think it important enough to warrant further investigation. Other happenings in Todd's life gradually emerged that gave hint of a troubled son who needed help.

Horrible nightmares would awaken Todd during his sleep.

Often they were so frightening and real that he would be literally trembling from head to foot. While he recovered from the dream, he typically would be in a trancelike state, seemingly neither awake nor asleep. Attempts to awaken him from the trance were fruitless, and though the eight-year-old boy would cling to his parents, they couldn't communicate with him. He seemed to be staring into the distance at some fearful scene.

At times Todd would talk in his sleep, and his speech was more than an occasional word or phrase. The talking seemed like conversations, though his parents could hear only one side of the conversation. These conversation times would awaken Todd and leave him fearful.

Prayer was vital to the recovery process. When Todd was awakened by these fearful experiences, his parents learned to immediately resort to authoritative prayer. Often as his parents prayed, Todd would suddenly cease his trembling and fall back to sleep.

Todd's story demonstrates some of the evidences of spiritistic activity a parent may observe in his child's life. I conduct spiritual warfare conferences at local churches, and at one I met Todd's parents, a couple I'll call the Joiners. They were drawn into spiritual warfare study through Todd's experiences. They both had felt an "evil presence" when their child awoke in sheer terror. Though they knew nothing about the subject, they together wondered if it could be demonic. They had looked for good reading on the subject in their local Christian bookstore and had been advised to read *The Adversary,* my first book on spiritual warfare. The Joiners thanked me, saying the book had helped them understand some principles of using one's authority to resist demonic attack. They had been aggressively using those principles and had seen Todd released from both his dreams and his imaginary friend.

The Joiners' experience introduces us to the practical benefits of biblically balanced spiritual warfare. Without psychological counseling or professional help of any kind, they had used spiritual principles to help their hurting son. Although not all problems that children have respond as quickly and effectively to biblical warfare as did Todd's, there is an important insight that needs to be emphasized. Spiritual resources demand a place of first priority in every believer's life. We have often looked too quickly to the secular world for answers to perplexing problems and have neglected the proper use of our weapons of warfare. Even when medical or psychological help may be needed to fully resolve a hurtful problem, the entire healing process will be enhanced by a proper use of our spiritual resources.

TODD'S "IMAGINARY FRIEND"

As they conversed with their son, Todd's parents concluded that his imaginary friend was actually a spirit entity who conversed with Todd as he played. At times Todd actually envisioned a "boylike figure." Usually he was good to Todd but other times he used threats to force and coerce him to do things that Todd didn't like. He also would appear at night in some of Todd's dreams and have troubling conversations that brought fear and confused thinking into Todd's life.

At first Todd was reluctant to give up his playtime friend, but prayer changed that. As his parents began to lead him in protective prayers at bedtime to claim God's shielding from intrusive demonic activity, two things happened. The horrible nightmares and terror experiences stopped. But Todd's play "friend" also became more abusive in his conversations with Todd. He expressed anger at Todd that their "secret" was known.

His parents instructed their son to command the "friend" to leave him in the name of the Lord Jesus Christ and to go where Jesus commanded him to go. With encouragement, he learned to resist this "friend" who had turned angry, and to use authority over him. To Todd's delight the abusive words stopped and the "friend" stopped his visits. What was becoming a trauma of fear was resolved by spiritual resources and a young boy was schooled in resisting his enemy.

A word of caution is in order. Please do not conclude that your child's imaginary friend must be a demon. My children and grandchildren have played with imaginary friends. I have never seen any evidence that demonic entities were involved in their experience. Make-believe friends can be part of a healthy playtime. Such fantasy shows a child's capacity for creativity through active imagination. We must always keep a proper balance in our perspective or our alertness may do unnecessary harm to the ones we long to protect.

How do you know when to suspect demonic influence? Communication is an important ingredient in evaluating whatever is happening in our children's lives. In Todd's case, communication began to reveal that something evil was occurring in their son's life. When they learned that their son's "friend" actually appeared at times and talked to Todd in threatening language, they knew something was not right. The accompanying terror dreams and trancelike states where they sensed an "evil" presence provided added evidence that protection was needed.

A WORD OF CAUTION

One hesitates in a chapter like this to suggest areas that may evidence spiritistic activity in the lives of our children. If you are skeptical that spiritistic activities will occur in your own child, good. If used wrongly, such "evidences" could lead us to seeing demons in everything that happens. We could fall into a condition of "spiritual neurosis," where we convey to our children a superstitious preoccupation with demons and wicked spirits. Young children would respond in fear to such parental imbalance, but as they grow older they might well dismiss the whole subject with a laugh of scorn. They could then dismiss the important subject of biblically balanced spiritual warfare as being a part of fanatical religion. Satan's ultimate strategy is to discredit any balanced teaching about how to resist him and his work. Wisdom, prudence, and prayerful quietness should be our first-line strategy in using warfare in behalf of our children.

However, having said that, please recognize that such influences can affect any child, yours or mine (as was the case with our daughter Judy). Yet let me urge caution as well. In my years of counseling, I can recall occasions where a concerned parent brought a troubled child to me, asking that I cast a demon out of him. That usually indicates that the parent has already conveyed to the child that he is demon possessed. There are few things that a parent could do to harm his child more and make him vulnerable to the deceiver's work. Such unwise communications convey false guilt, rejection, and diminished self-worth to a child.

The child gains this impression: "My parents think I'm really bad and the Devil has me. I'm no good and I'll never be worth anything." The Devil's helpers reinforce that faulty perception of self-worth by using all of the deceptive tools available to them.

Children are highly impressionable, and parents must maintain a constant, protective sensitivity as they help them through their hurts. Even when there is strong evidence of demonic control in a child's life, it's best not to work directly with the child in any kind of confrontation procedures. Christian parents can guard their child's freedom. As parents consistently exercise their God-given position of protective authority in their child's life, even the most resistant strongholds of evil will be forced to retreat. Grandparents and even close Christian friends can also exercise their protective authority by watching over a troubled child in prayer.

KEEPING A BIBLICAL BALANCE

Todd's parents provided a model for parental intervention in their child's life. Without alarming Todd and by careful reading, they learned how to exercise biblically balanced spiritual warfare. Prayer intervention stopped the trancelike stupors at night. Pre-sleep protective prayer ended the intrusive nightmare activity of the powers of darkness in his dreams. Subconscious conversations during sleep with his make-believe "friend" also ceased. Through prayer and patient communication, the Lord opened the door for them to introduce their son to biblical resistance of spiritistic activity without frightening or harming him. They showed a spiritual wisdom that deserves emulation.

Cathy was not so fortunate. She experienced nightmare dreams and behavior patterns that caused her parents to suspect spiritual oppression. They took Cathy when she was seven to a highly charged healing meeting, hoping to gain help for her. The healer professed to have the gift of "discernment" and the ability to miraculously heal and cast out demons. In a highly emotional state, the mystical healer laid hands on Cathy, named the demon, and commanded him to leave her. Cathy fell to the floor in a trancelike state and was pronounced delivered from the demon.

Years later, a now-grown Cathy sat across from me to explain how the whole experience had left her with fears and torments that she was afraid to share with her parents. She was fearful that they might take her to such a meeting again. Cathy felt the experience had contributed to a downward path for her. As she matured in years, Cathy chose her own way to heal her hurts. She tried to forget and find help in pleasure. She drew away from her parents and her church. Rebellion, sinful living, and occult experimentation had worked together to bring her life into a shambles of confusion and deeper bondage to powers of darkness. She hurt so much that she finally turned to the Lord in her pain. She had come to seek help to gain her freedom from the powers of darkness that tormented her.

What does Cathy's experience tell us? Does it mean that we ought never to go to a healing meeting? Of course not. A pattern for divine healing is commended in James 5. Many of us have experienced miraculous healings that have occurred in our local church, in a hospital when we were desperately ill, or even in our own home as fellow believers came and prayed over us. God's power to miraculously heal must never be doubted or opposed.

Cathy's experience does say that we must be very careful in how we seek that healing, especially as we experience end-time conditions and events. The Word of God has specifically warned us that one of the chief manifestations of end-time deception will be "counterfeit miracles, signs and wonders" (2 Thessalonians 2:9, cf. vv. 10–12). Other passages like Matthew 7:21–23, Matthew 24:24–25, and Revelation 13:13–14 remind us of the counterfeit miraculous works that will be a part of the end-time deceptions. These works will be so deceiving that even some who do the miracle works apparently will not realize that they are using occult healing powers (Matthew 7:21–23). The deceptions will be so clever that Jesus warned that even God's very elect might be deceived if that were possible (Matthew 24:24).

Since we are living in a day where many are emphasizing the supernatural, wisdom and caution need to be practiced by the Lord's people. Eastern religions, New Age mysticism, and outright satanism all utilize evil supernaturalism to effect healings that appear miraculous. It's a time to exercise prayerful caution. Unlike some Christian leaders (some of whom are my personal friends), I do not believe this is a day where we should be promoting "signs and wonders" to authenticate our message.

If our Lord Jesus Christ by His sovereign plan chooses to grant miraculous happenings in these times, we all will rejoice in His purposes. However, promoting the possibility of miracles happening to enlarge meeting attendance or to authenticate the message we proclaim is unwise for the age in which we live. Counterfeit miracles and wonders are to be the chief tools that Satan uses in his last thrust to deceive the masses and rule the world. He is already using that appeal in a broad spectrum of deception.

The authentication of the gospel has already been firmly established. The death, burial, and resurrection of our Lord Jesus Christ authenticates the message we proclaim. History affirms that truth. By divine revelation, we have it fully recorded in all of its detail in our Bibles. We need no more than that. Everyone who has been saved thus far came to Christ because of that gospel message, and everyone who will be saved will come for the same reason. (See Romans 1:16 and 1 Corinthians 15:1–11.)

ANGELS ON OUR SIDE

The created spirit beings called angels were all holy and righteous in the original creation. By God's direct creative act each angel was made for God's intended purpose. God created angels with different levels of rank, authority, and power, and had a specific purpose for each one. (See Ephesians 6:12; Colossians 1:16–17.) Lucifer may have been created to be the most powerful of all the angelic host. He most certainly was one of the lead ranking angels. The biblical evidence seems to indicate that only the archangel, Michael, and possibly Gabriel were created with an equal rank and authority to Satan.

When Satan, or Lucifer as Isaiah names him, rebelled against God, he drew one-third of the created angels into his rebellious scheme to take over God's position (Revelation 12:1–4; see also the chapter 6 outline, "Redeemed Man Facing the World and Satan's Kingdom"). These fallen angels, or spirit beings, continue to function in their created rank and authority but now instead of doing the will of the true and living God, they serve the Devil.

All angels were created to minister, to serve God in His sovereign purpose and "those who will inherit salvation" (Hebrews 1:14) as their main focus. Angels are to "guard you in all your ways" (Psalm 91:11; see also vv. 12–15). Since Satan and his followers rebelled against their position, the demonic hosts, or evil angels, work to destroy God's kingdom and undermine the witness and ministry of those who follow Jesus Christ. But let us remember that God has a twofold purpose designed for holy angels and their ministry to God's redeemed ones. These good angels guard the abiding, redeemed ones from the hurtful schemes of Satan's kingdom to harm protected believers. They also assist protected believers to walk in triumphant victory over the schemes of Satan's work and workers. Jesus told His earliest followers: "I have given you authority to trample on snakes and scorpions and to overcome all the power of the enemy" (Luke 10:19). It is in God's plans to crush Satan under the feet of believers (Romans 16:20).

Satan uses the fallen angels to try to rob us of our freedom and destroy us (John 10:10), but the holy angels continue to minister and protect. Those good angels are God's resources to us that we should not ignore.

A spiritual battle is underway between the fallen angels and the holy ones. It's all-out war. Just as the major work of holy angels is to minister to and care for the redeemed, the major activity of the fallen angels is to attack, defeat, and destroy the redeemed.[1] Those who follow Jesus will find the

challenge to live holy in the world will involve a spiritual struggle at times, what the apostle Paul calls a wrestling match in
Ephesians 6:12.

My purpose in reminding us of the ministry of angels at
this point is to illustrate again why parents need to be on their
guard in this spiritistic age. There is a diabolical conspiracy of
unseen spirit beings determined to rob, kill, and destroy us and
our children. Our protective resources are awesome in God's
grace, but we must not passively assume that protection. We
are responsible to aggressively use those resources to wisely
assist and protect our children.

EVIDENCES OF SPIRITISTIC
ACTIVITY IN OUR CHILDREN

With these cautions and resources in mind, the question
remains: How can we recognize spiritistic activity in our children's lives? Here is a list of twenty-two signs. Still, the listing is
not exhaustive; there may well be other evidences that I have
neglected to mention. Furthermore, the listing is not conclusive.
If one or more of these signs appear in your child, do not automatically conclude that spirit powers are trying to rule and
destroy your son or daughter. The appearance in your child of
several of these *may* mean your child is under attack. A combi-
nation of evidences should cause us to pray more directly and
authoritatively to watch over our children and victoriously
"wrestle" in their behalf.

Abnormal Fears and Phobias

Fear is probably the Devil's chief weapon of attack. I have
often said that fear toward Satan can be compared to faith
toward God. Faith pleases and activates the Lord's response
toward those who belong to Him. Without faith it is impossible
to please God, but faith toward the Lord pleases Him greatly
(see Hebrews 11, especially v. 6). Fear activates and pleases the
Devil because it is the direct antithesis to faith. The lion roars
to make his victims fearful and Satan roars like a lion to victim-
ize us (1 Peter 5:8). When a child's life is characterized by a

trembling fear about many things, one sees suspicious evidence of the Devil's work. When Satan's work is defeated in that person's life the element of fear usually comes quickly back into balance.

Abnormal fears in our children should prompt an observant parent to begin to focus prayer against any demonic powers of fear that are seeking to rule that child. Early resistance to such ruling tactics may well save a child from what could become a spiritistic rule of fear.

Out-of-Control Anger and "Fits of Rage" Behavior Patterns

Anger, even "fits of rage" anger, appears in some form in each of the New Testament lists that catalogue the sins of the flesh (See Matthew 15:9–20; Mark 7:20–23; Galatians 5:19–21; Colossians 3:5–14.) Ephesians 4:26–27, however, warns that the willful practice of anger does "give place to the devil." Anger that controls you can be a symptom of a spirit of anger or rage beginning to exercise ruling control over the person.

Ned was an angry little boy. Big for his age, he began to manipulate and control his mother through his violent rages. If she failed to give him what he wanted, he would often resort to a tirade of out-of-control anger. He would beat on her with his fists and kick at her with his heavy shoes. Discipline was totally ineffective. It only made his rages worse. It wasn't until his mother recognized that she was dealing with more than an angry son that Ned began to change. Her consistent prayer against the attempt of a spirit of anger to rule over her son began to free him up and eliminate his outbursts of rage and violence against her.

Seeing Apparitions in the Room or Hearing Voices

Tom, the young son of a pastor, would often come in sheer terror into his parents' room complaining of seeing sinister faces that grinned at him in the dark. Thinking that their son was just having a nightmare, the parents would have him crawl into bed with them until he fell back to sleep. The father would then carry Tom back to his own bed and usually he would sleep through the rest of the night. The occurrence of these fearful experiences began to increase until one night the little fellow complained that there were "two of them." Still convinced that it was just a nightmare and the over-active imagination of his boy, the father walked his son back to the room. As they neared the door, the father heard voices in the room and began to feel cold chills sweep over him. As he pushed the door open, he told of seeing two dark, shadowlike figures quickly disappear.

Kneeling by his son's bed, that pastor-father prayed with his son for the Lord's guarding protection against such apparition appearances in his son's room. A consistent practice of warfare prayer saw the elimination of such unwelcome "visits" from the realm of darkness.

That dramatic account is beyond the experience of most believers. It was a part of a larger picture of the spiritual warfare experiences coming at that time to a Christian leader and his family. The Lord used it to train them to help others under attack. Their experience does remind us not to dismiss too quickly a child's account of an "appearance" of some sort or voices speaking when no one is around.

If the child is very young, it would seem best for the parent to not make much over it in the child's presence. Taking up a protective prayer approach, the parent should forbid all powers of darkness from making any spiritistic visits. It's appropriate to also ask the Lord to assign His holy angels to guard against such offensive intrusion into the home and the life of one's child. As mentioned earlier, such protective prayer is extremely effective and devastates the plans of darkness. (See the sample prayer under "For a Child Hearing Voices, Etc." in chapter 11.)

When a child has received the Lord Jesus Christ and is greater in maturity, intrusive spiritistic activity can provide an opportunity for training that child in resisting the Devil and his schemes. Spirit powers try to rule through fear and foreboding. The appearance of an apparition would frighten most adult Christians, let alone a child. Yet, a careful, prayerful approach to help a child know his authority to resist, and to equip him with words to say, can serve a wonderful purpose.

It's extremely important in this spiritistic age to not be intimidated by experiences that have a supernatural aura about them. These kinds of happenings seem to be increasing. Knowing what to do eliminates the fear of the unknown and enables a wise parent to use all experiences for the maturing and spiritual development of children.

Cruel Treatment of Animals or Playmates

King David prayed, "Consider my enemies, for they are many; and they hate me with cruel hatred" (Psalm 25:19, NKJV). As David mentions these many enemies, he refers to their use of brutal cruelty; he might be referring to the realm of supernatural evil. Cruelty is a part of most forms of evil, but it has particular significance when you face the Devil.

Those who counsel the demonically oppressed are repeatedly reminded concerning what a ruthlessly cruel enemy the Devil is. Remember that cruelty is the very antithesis of Christ and the fruit of the Holy Spirit. One of the most beautiful characteristics of the Lord Jesus is His gentleness (Matthew 11:29; Philippians 4:5). Extreme forms of cruelty may indicate occult influence.

One of the strongest evidences of Satan's rule is cruelty. Those who counsel a satanic ritual abuse (SRA) victim soon learn that cruelty is the name of the game for satanists. Upon hearing the recalled memories of SRA victims, most counselors struggle with disbelief. Though wanting to honor their client's integrity of memory, the cruelty level described by the victim seems incredible to the average person.

My experience has been that most people who come out of satanism and SRA do so because they suffer and hurt so much. The Devil rules by the cruel hurt he puts on people. They must keep going deeper into cultish wickedness or the powers of darkness tighten the screws of suffering. The only relief comes when they conform.

Perhaps that's enough to suggest why cruelty to animals or hurtful conduct toward siblings or playmate friends should be cause for concern. Oppressive activity from the cruel powers of darkness may indicate an effort to manipulate a child to their kind of ruthlessness.

A Controlling Conduct of Hate

Hate is the antithesis of love. The apostle John wrote: "Whoever does not love does not know God, because God is love" (1 John 4:8). To say that "Satan is hate" fits both his fallen character and his determined function. He seeks to rule by hate.

Little Jennifer didn't like to be corrected at all but if parental correction included even a mild form of discipline, she usually erupted with expressions of hate. Her hatred usually focused on her mother. A dark countenance would come over her as she clenched her teeth and screamed out, "I hate you! I hate you! I hate you!"

When such conduct lengthened the discipline of a time-out confinement to a chair, Jennifer would turn the hatred toward herself. Her mother would hear her muttering: "I hate myself! I hate my looks! I hate my room!"

Sometimes her mother could bring her out of it by reading a book to her or playing a game with her. Yet, the feelings of hate were always close to the surface. If anything displeased Jennifer, the hate scenario would start afresh. Her mother confided, "When I see that hatred in her eyes, it frightens me."

Jennifer's parents knew there was something abnormal about their daughter's preoccupation with hatred, but they linked it with the Devil's work only after reading Neil Anderson's book, *The Seduction of Our Children*.[2] The parents began patterns of prayerful intercession and spiritual solutions. As they witnessed the changes taking place in their daughter in response to their application of warfare principles, they had no doubt that Jennifer had been under demonic assault.

Like cruelty, strong hatred arises from satanic influence and involvement. Jennifer's parents were young Christian parents but wise to recognize the source of their daughter's hatred. When I asked them if I might share some of their intimate family pain while keeping their identity confidential, their response was enthusiastic.

"Please do!" they said. "If any other parents are hurting like we were in helpless frustration and defeat, tell them to get involved in spiritual warfare. It saved our lives."

Other Evidences of Spiritistic Activity

The remaining evidences of spiritistic activity in children are no less important than the first five. In fact, some of them may be even more symptomatic of wicked spirit oppression than those first listed. But we will not elaborate as much, because of space limitations and some overlapping of the evidences. I trust that the relevancy of this listing is becoming self-evident. The presence of one or more of these evidences in a child's life may well mean that parents need to learn and practice the warfare principles that Jennifer's parents learned.

Trancelike states of sleep. Sleep walking, sleep talking, or conversations while in a sleep trance that are not remembered when the child finally awakens are suspect. Even bed wetting while a child is in a trance sleep pattern could signal spiritistic sleep control. Please don't conclude that I think all bed wetting to be of demonic origin. Physiological, psychological, and medical reasons must be carefully considered as well as spiritual. Similarly, a person who talks in his sleep is not necessarily communicating with demons.

Compulsive behavior patterns. Compulsive lying, stealing, cursing, hitting, fighting, laughing, crying, pinching, pounding of head on the wall, or cutting oneself with a sharp object are but a few of the compulsive actions children may exhibit. Compulsive behavior patterns could signal control that is not originating in the child's own person.

Physical symptoms that defy medical diagnosis or treatment and may change or vary in kind and degree. Pains that vary in intensity and move from one part of the body to another, pressure feelings around the eyes or a tight band sensation around the head, dizzy spells where everything in the room seems to be spinning, numbness in the extremities or in certain spots on the skin surface, tic facial sensations, epilepsy-type seizures that do not show up as epilepsy in medical tests, jerking actions or feelings in the arms or legs, uncomfortable sensations of someone touching the genital or rectal areas, and feelings that someone is choking you—these are some of the physical symptoms that may indicate demonic activity. I have personally witnessed counselees becoming free from these physical symptoms as they learned to use their authority to resist the spiritistic oppression causing the symptom.

Physical symptoms like the above always merit medical diagnosis and attention. Though the prayerful application of spiritual principles is always in order, wise balance demands that symptoms such as those described receive competent medical evaluation. They could indicate the onset of physical need or disease. Failure to recognize that fact could jeopardize the health of the one experiencing the symptom.

A preoccupation with blood, death, feces, fire, or violence. Billy seemed to be attracted to feces from his infancy. He smeared it on everything when he had the chance. Later, interests in blood and fire seemed to virtually control him. Any violence on TV would cause him to stop what he was doing and rush to see the gore. These were important clues together with others that evidenced spiritual oppression on Billy. Parental spiritual warfare had to be applied before Billy showed relief from these destructive patterns.

Clairvoyant and ESP "gifts" that emerge in a child's life. Premonitions, abilities in extrasensory perception (ESP) or supernatural "gifts" that emerge in our children should always be suspect and never encouraged. Such gifts usually are generational and signal occult activity that was practiced by some family member in the generational lineage.

Cutting or hurting of self and certain instances of accident proneness. Those troubled by the powers of darkness often resort to actions that bring self-hurt to them. Cutting of themselves with razor blades or knives is as old as the biblical accounts. (See Mark 5; 1 Kings 18:28.) Some cases of accident or injury proneness may signal the same kind of hurtful desire expressed in a subtle form.

Withdrawal from family and friends and a loner mentality. A desire to be alone has its healthy expressions. Time for reflection, meditation, study, and prayer produces emotional, mental, and spiritual benefit. Unhealthy expressions are displayed when accompanied by moody anger, rejection of loved ones, loneliness, suspicion, and fear. Extreme fanaticizing about imaginary friends, places, and events often accompany this move into isolation and withdrawal. Especially when children want to avoid family and friends, such alienation can indicate demonic deception at work.

Inability to concentrate and learn even when average and above-average abilities are evident. The inability of the human mind to receive or express information can signal the works of darkness. God is not the author of confusion, but the Devil delights to produce confusion; he will impair understanding in every way he can. Hyperactive distraction may be a part of enemy effort to interfere with concentration and learning. When a child is medically diagnosed as being hyperactive, in addition to medication, protective warfare prayer should be regularly used by the Christian parents.

Overt interest in ghosts, magic, occultism, fortune-telling and similar fare. The kingdom of darkness has certain tools that it uses against humanity to gain advantage and opportunity for control and rule. Occult activity in its many forms—from black magic to fortune-telling—is a regular tool the Enemy uses. Subtle interests on the part of a child in such fare may signal the manipulative attempt of wicked spirits to gain ground against a child. A child's interest in clever illusions, however, usually indicates only a delight in being fooled. If he watches a bunny disappear and then reappear, or observes a woman being "sawn" in half, he or she may desire to "figure out the trick." This is not the same as seeking after black magic that tries to control and overpower other people and the world around him.

Perverted sexual interests or activity even before puberty. Perverted sexuality and the control of darkness always go hand in hand. Early masturbation, pornography interest, and sensual talk may signal the invisible works of evil powers. Often the child becomes obsessed and seems controlled by these desires.

Inability to give or accept gestures of kindness and love. Healthy human interaction includes the giving and receiving of love. When a child rejects love, that usually signals an emotional problem, but it may signal demonic influence. God is love, and as previously mentioned, Satan has no part in love. He hates. The practice of warfare prayer and principles should be aggressively applied when a child can neither accept nor give out love.

Destructive acts. Satan and his workers are destroyers. Children being subtly manipulated and maneuvered by powers of darkness may manifest destructive behavior. If children deliberately break things and destroy their toys, etc., the behavior may indicate influence from evil, destructive powers. In some cases, children will even smash toys that previously they treated as personal treasures.

Extreme depression and expressed thoughts about suicide. Suicide remains one of the major causes of death among children and young people. Psychologists, sociologists, and others expressing professional concern about this disturbing increase cite a major spectrum of causes. Jesus once ascribed to Satan the role of murderer. Here are His startling words, addressed to His critics who were out to take His life:

> You belong to your father, the devil, and you want to carry out your father's desire. He was a murderer from the beginning, not holding to the truth, for there is no truth in him. When he lies, he speaks his native language, for he is a liar and the father of lies. (John 8:44)

When anyone takes his own life, I am convinced that the work of the deceiver and the murderer is at work. He has "the power of death," according to Hebrews 2:14. The normal human desire built into us by our Creator is to live.

Sleep problems. While counseling an obviously demonized person, one will frequently face yawning and great sleepiness on the part of the counselee. He experiences similar sleepiness when the Bible is being read, prayer is being offered, or some important truth is being discussed. While counseling people afflicted in that way, I've even noted sleepiness trying to overtake me. Usually offering a resisting prayer will quickly stop such obvious attempts of oppressive interference. Other sleep problems can be bad dreams, restless tossing during sleep, and even an inability to sleep (insomnia). Sleep problems in children can usually be remedied by proper protective prayer before they go to sleep.

A hateful, rebellious response toward corrective discipline. Corrective discipline is both commanded by God and practiced by our loving heavenly Father (see Proverbs 13:24; Hebrews 12:1–15). The rejection of discipline may well suggest the nefarious activity of some evil influence. Sometimes children respond with hate to discipline that is fair and much deserved; such a rebellious response may be triggered by spiritistic influences.

Inability to enjoy play, laughter, and fun games. Fun, play, games, and laughter are almost as natural to children as breathing. No sooner did the bombs and rocket shellings cease in Sarajevo than the children were out in the streets to laugh and play, even in the rubble. When a child cannot enjoy a fun game, something very dark is going on. Satan seeks to rob children of their laughter. Even a superficial investigation of the SRA activities of the cultists informs us of how darkness wants to steal away all wholesome fun and laughter of children.

The appearance of occult and satanic symbols on a child's books, clothing, possessions or body. Satan may harass and trouble the lives of our children in many and varied ways, but his end goal is to make them willing participants in his programs of evil. He seeks to draw them into magical, mystical interests and overt experimentation with supernatural evil. The purpose of this book is not to develop an extensive study of occultism. Others have provided helpful information about this evil.[3] Every parent should develop sufficient awareness of Satan's entrapments to know the evidences of even superficial interests on the part of his or her child.

It's always very subtle at first. Occult and satanic symbols may begin to appear on a child's notebooks, clothing, hands, arms, or face. Interest in heavy metal rock music is usually a part of early stages. Books, tapes, or articles about seances, curses, rituals, and magical potions are a part of the reading materials of one being drawn into supernatural evil.

The Proper Response to Spiritistic Activity in Children

As a parent, you may observe one or more of these evidences of possible spiritistic influence mentioned above. If that happens, what do you do? Here are five suggestions for dealing with possible demonic activity in your child's life:

1. Be calm and do not fear. Fear is a chief tool of Satan to rule and destroy. He will relentlessly try to upset you and thus your child. Don't panic and display frantic concern. Remember, the Lord Jesus Christ has given each born-again believer all the power and authority needed to overcome darkness and protect our children.

2. Keep a biblical balance. Remember Cathy's parents? Don't seek out a "faith healer" or "expert in spiritual warfare" to cast out demons from your child. That sensational approach, as noted earlier, can be very harmful to a child. Furthermore, it typically is looking for a quick fix. Instead, seek a biblically balanced approach as you apply spiritual truth and parental protection to your child.

3. Express your concerns to your pastor if he has spiritual insights and a growing understanding of biblical spiritual warfare. Describe the battle and enlist his prayer support. Careful counsel from him may provide important insights.

4. Use biblical warfare praying on a daily basis. The prayers appearing in the final chapter offer helpful guidance and insights on how to use your authority to resist the Enemy.

5. Make your own private list of suspicious evidences of spiritistic activity against your child. This is helpful for your times of prayerful intercession. It can also assist in addressing directly your parental authority against powers of darkness.

Before you use this final suggestion to confront the power of darkness through prayer, prepare yourself spiritually. Prepare your own heart with a day of fasting and prayer for the Lord to grant you the wisdom and courage to use your authority in Christ to free your child from the harassment of the powers of darkness. As a parent, you may want to go through the steps to freedom (see next chapter).

6. Select a time when quiet, uninterrupted prayer focus can be maintained for at least thirty minutes. If your bedroom is in the general proximity of the sleeping child, that may be the best place and time for such a direct confrontation. If both parents are together and Christians, come together in prayer; but a single parent need not be fearful. It's our Lord's authority and not our numbers that brings about the protection and freedom.

A sample payer for addressing possible demonic influence on your child is included as Appendix 2. I recommend you use it or develop a similar specific prayer for protection against any powers of darkness you suspect of harassing your child. The prayer calls upon Jesus to bind such spiritistic forces and to remove any lingering forces of evil that could deceive your child. The prayer also calls upon the Holy Spirit to sanctify the child's whole person for service.

Addressing truth and the believer's authority to resist evil activity in this way honors God and weakens evil. Accompanied with the steps of freedom and other procedures in this book, the freeing process will be effective and powerful. Parents may want to use this procedure on more than one occasion. Doors of opportunity for enemy activity must be closed. Continuing watchfulness is the Lord's command (Ephesians 6:18).

CHAPTER TEN

APPLYING THE STEPS TO FREEDOM

The transfer of blessings—and of disasters—from one generation to the next makes a fascinating study in the Old Testament. The biblical accounts make the linkage between the previous generation's action and the descendants' behavior quite clear. This is seen especially in biblical records of the kings of Israel and Judah, who ruled from after Solomon to the captivity that overcame Israel and later Judah. Bad kings spawned more bad kings; breaking the mold was not easy. Among the rulers of Judah only five kings fully honored God after Solomon; most were influenced to evil by the waywardness of their parents.

When the king served God in a pleasing manner, almost without exception the generational tie is made to David, the man after God's own heart, or some other God-fearing man in the king's generational lineage. For instance, twice in 2 Chronicles, a good king is compared with King David: "He did what was right in the eyes of the Lord, just as his father David had done" (29:2; 34:2). When a king followed sinful ways, a link often can be found to someone wicked in the king's generational lineage. The Scripture is very careful to make this tie. For instance, "Amon was twenty-two years old when he became king, and he reigned in Jerusalem two years. He did evil in the sight of the Lord, as his father Manasseh had done" (2 Chronicles 33:21–22).

This linkage to the generational flow often is associated with a parent's conduct and faith. Wickedness and disobedience seem to transfer the sins of one to the child in direct lineage or to some other evildoers of the human lineage. Faith, obedience, and godly conduct almost always have a direct generational tie to the godly in the family tree.

Perhaps as a parent, you worry that the sins and rebelliousness of your own parents or previous generations have affected your life as well as your ability to rear your children to godliness. How do I begin to undo all of the rubble from my personal and family failures? Your concern is a good sign, showing your desire to change. Surely change is possible as a child of God. Such change can give you both the resources and the examples that your children desire as they grow toward adulthood. How do you do that?

CHANGE CAN OCCUR

Before we answer that question, let me assure you that such change can occur. As noted earlier, the transfer of ancestral wickedness or generational godliness is not automatic or irreversible. The patterns of earlier generations are not like original sin. This is in line with individual responsibility and the constant opportunity a loving God provides for repentance and grace.

Let's return to the long line of kings in the Old Testament to demonstrate this. Manasseh, one of the later kings of Judah, was perhaps its most wicked. Through His prophets the Lord said, "Manasseh . . . has done more evil than the Amorites who preceded him . . ." (2 Kings 21:11). The catalogue of his sins includes such abominable practices as sacrificing his sons to the heathen gods in the Valley of the Son of Hinnom, a form of Molech worship. The worst forms of witchcraft, sorcery, fortune-telling, and occult magical practices were promoted by Manasseh. To add insult toward God, he even brought his wickedness into the sacred temple set apart to worship the God of Israel. In his folly, we read that he "led Judah and the people of Jerusalem astray, so that they did more evil than the nations the Lord had destroyed before the Israelites" (2 Chronicles 33:9).

Despite such evil, the Lord showed great patience with Manasseh. Although the text doesn't say why, I think God's patience came because of the godly life of his father, the good King Hezekiah. We even see the mercy of God displayed in the way the Lord deals with this very wicked king. The Assyrian army invades Judah. Manasseh is captured and is led away in disgrace with a chain hooked in his nose and his hand tightly bound with brass shackles.

In a brief but graphic description, a marvelous testimony to God's gracious goodness is recorded:

> In his distress, he sought the favor of the Lord his God and humbled himself greatly before the God of his fathers. And when he prayed to him, the Lord was moved by his entreaty and listened to his plea; so he brought him back to Jerusalem and to his kingdom. Then Manasseh knew that the Lord is God. (2 Chronicles 33:12–13)

Manasseh followed up his restoration with a thorough cleanup of the wicked things he had done in Jerusalem, the temple, and throughout the nation of Judah. Repentance saved his reign from total disaster. He finished his long rule with comparative prosperity and peace. When he died the nation gave him an honorable burial and put his son, Amon, on the throne.

Amon's reign lasted only two years. The wicked ways he'd learned from his father were the practice of his life. No repentance, however, was ever forthcoming. Finally he was assassinated by his own household servants, and his eight-year-old son, Josiah, was installed on Judah's throne. Josiah was a godly king who instituted one of the greatest reforms that the nation had experienced since the days of Samuel and David.

The history of Hezekiah and his descendants proves the point: Generational sin, no matter how wicked, can be reversed and forgiven. Genuine repentance is the key. Even a Manasseh found forgiveness and miraculous restoration through God's grace. The scars of his sins corrupted his son's reign, but Manasseh's late-life faith and prayers and those of his father, Hezekiah, brought generational blessings. Their respective grandson and great-grandson, Josiah, was one of Judah's most godly reformers.

The healing power resulting from saving faith, godly repentance, and believing prayer finds no scars or obstacles too large to be removed. Neither generational sin nor any other kinds of wickedness can cancel the power of the gospel to liberate, transform, and turn generational curses into blessings.

Regardless of your personal or generational background, healing, forgiveness, and freedom are to be found in God's grace and mercy. The furthermost reaches of wickedness and evil can be conquered and the generational consequences forever removed by the finished work of Christ. This chapter looks at how to apply that freedom to yourself so that you may raise your children in a home of spiritual strength.

A PLACE TO BEGIN

Where does one begin to apply his freedom? You may have started so well in your Christian commitment to Christ, but now the joy has faded. Your peace has gone. You're wondering where you missed it. Why all the stress? Defeats and the trash of failures clutter up your life. It's almost like you've lost your way. Even though you're fairly confident about your salvation, your walk is all messed up in sinful defeats. The problem may be linked to the influences of past generations; even if it is not, you want to change your sinful patterns so you can rear your children in a godly home.

In chapter 12 of *The Bondage Breaker,*[1] Neil T. Anderson's fine book on spiritual warfare, Anderson presents several steps to freedom. I highly recommend the book, which can help every Christian who will read it carefully. I believe that the greatest use for these steps to freedom will be realized when God brings revival awakening to His church. The perverted sexual sins, widespread occultism, abusive parenting, drug usage, homes broken by divorce, and so many of today's sins have opened many people's lives to demonic afflictions of varying degrees. When those with such backgrounds come to know Jesus Christ as Savior and Lord, disciplers would do converts a great service by helping each go through the steps to freedom.

Let me present an adaptation of Anderson's freedom steps. They may help you as a parent find freedom as you help lead your children into spiritual maturity. They may also help when a fellow believer struggling with these issues comes to you for help. A word of qualification: Demonic harassment of a tormenting nature in a believer's life is abnormal. It can happen only when serious ground has been given to the kingdom of darkness. The struggles you or your child are facing may not be spiritistic in nature. But when ground has been given to the enemy, it must be renounced. By patient counseling, the surrendered ground can usually be discovered; but it is often a painful and tedious process. The steps to freedom can greatly facilitate this process.

STEPS TO FREEDOM

The freedom steps cover the major areas and ways that believers give ground to darkness. Parents will do well to go through the steps to freedom for their own spiritual benefit. There may also be times when they will need to lead their child or youth through these important steps. We are speaking of a delicate matter. We cannot force such action on our child. If a child is threatened because of the parent-child relationship, a youth pastor, Sunday school teacher, or godly friend may be the one to help.

One can go through the steps alone, but we've found that the presence of a spiritually alert counselor or friend is of major benefit. The prayer support, protective assistance, and confidentiality provide the proper spiritual atmosphere.

Proper Preparation

A quiet place relatively free from the possibility of interruption is most desirable. A time frame of two to three hours may be necessary. A hurried atmosphere must be avoided.

Prior preparation should include opportunity to work through each area, making a list of all matters that need to be examined. Some may wish to precede the session by a period of prayer and fasting.

Believers also should assure themselves of the importance of this procedure. Finding freedom from demonic influence is important for two reasons. First, it gives us personal freedom. Many believers have given ground to the kingdom of darkness by past sinful practices. It is a spiritually healthful exercise to systematically confess and renounce these areas giving demonic powers claim against us. Repentance is a noble practice. It honors God and frees people.

Second, knowing the procedure gives us a transferable tool. The areas of need are so large that every believer must become equipped to help another believer claim his stand in the freedom Christ has won for him.

An Essential Foundation

Before beginning, we must be sure the proper foundation exists. Each participant in a freedom session must be sure that personal salvation is a by-faith reality. Are you trusting Jesus Christ alone for the forgiveness of your sins and the assurance of eternal life? I often urge those besieged by doubts to answer Satan's accusations with a positive affirmation of this type: "I affirm that my only hope for the forgiveness of my sins and the gaining of eternal life is resting upon the finished work of my Lord Jesus, and I trust my eternal destiny fully into His hands and to the sealing ministry of the Holy Spirit."

Here are three preliminary steps to follow to secure a good foundation before using the seven steps to freedom. First, ask the one you are helping the two excellent questions of the Evangelism Explosion program. Answering those questions can give the one we are ministering to (or yourself) a clear understanding of whether he has saving faith. The two questions are:

- "Have you come to the place in your spiritual life where you know for certain that if you were to die today, you'd go to heaven?" If the answer is positive, the next question will help you and the person understand where he is resting his faith.
- "If you should die and stand before the Lord and He were to ask, 'Why should I let you into my heaven?' what would you say?" Watch for a works-related answer. If the answer is not clear, take the time to carefully clarify God's plan of salvation. Campus Crusade's "Four Spiritual Laws" booklet or some other method of clarifying the gospel should be pursued. A clear understanding of saving faith is necessary before proceeding through the steps to freedom.

Second, after leading a person to saving faith, lead him/her through a renunciation prayer of this kind: "In the name of my Lord Jesus Christ and by the power of His blood, I here and now renounce and disown all those ways in which I have given any ground to Satan and his demon powers. I ask my Lord Jesus Christ to evict from my life any controlling powers of darkness and to send them where they may never control or trouble me again."

Third, watch for the new believer experiencing any adverse sensations or spiritual attacks as the renunciation is verbalized. Such attacks may indicate adverse demonic reaction to the renunciation. Going through the steps to freedom should be given first-priority significance if negative reactions are experienced.

THE SEVEN STEPS TO FREEDOM

As you proceed through the steps to freedom, severe demonic assault may try to manifest. It is usually wise to not allow this to happen. As a manifestation begins to emerge, use an authoritative command such as this:

> *In the name of my Lord Jesus Christ I forbid any demonic mani-*
> *festation that is attempting to interfere with this renunciation. By*
> *the power of the blood of the Lord Jesus Christ, I keep you sub-*
> *dued and unable to manifest in any way while I am working*
> *through this renunciation process.*

Helping the person verbalize the resistance command is advisable if you are assisting another person through the steps. Taking short phrases of the command and asking the counselee to repeat them after you is the best way to help him get through it. The process will also be teaching the believer how to use his authority over darkness in biblical application.

I am presenting the following seven steps in outline in order to assist those seeking to use these steps as a format of procedure.

Step 1: Renounce All Past Involvements

Step 1 is to *renounce all involvements with false religions, occult practices, divinations, magic, sorcery, witchcraft, spiritis-tic healings, séances, and similar activities* (Deuteronomy 18:9–14; Ephesians 5:8–14).

The questionnaire checklist in Appendix 3 can assist in the search process. Do not dismiss any exposure as insignificant. The most trivial dabbling may have opened the door to the harassment of the enemy. Prayer for the Lord to grant remembrance of all significant matters that need renunciation should be offered frequently as one works through each step. Here is a sample prayer: "I ask the Lord Jesus Christ to enable me to recall any and all spiritistic activities or false religious practices that have given any claim against me by the powers of darkness."

I. Renounce forgotten involvements.

  A. Spiritistic acts and false religious rituals may have been performed by well-meaning family members or others that have left a spiritistic claim against you. There may be other reasons for having forgotten very significant acts that have left their cloud of harm:

1. Spiritistic rituals at birth or in infancy.

2. Satanic ritual abuse activities in which you may have been forced to participate as a young child.

3. Any repressed memories too traumatic to remember that gave the enemy ground (deaths, fears, injuries, etc.).

4. Spiritistic healing practices in infancy or childhood to which you may have been exposed.

B. Renounce such involvements, even though forgotten, through prayer. Use the following model prayer:

Lord Jesus Christ, I confess that I may have been involved in harmful religious rituals and spiritistic practices that may have taken place which I do not now remember. I renounce all such forgotten involvements and I ask You to sever any claims of darkness upon me because of such involvement. I ask my Lord Jesus Christ to claim back all ground Satan's kingdom may be claiming in such things.

II. Renounce all remembered involvements.

A. Make a list of all those things the Holy Spirit enables you to remember that have to do with spiritistic acts of false religious rituals in which you participated.

B. Examine prayerfully a checklist (such as those shown at the beginning of this step).

C. Be ready to examine questionable areas; i.e., taking off one's shoes at a religious shrine may seem like a cultural custom to you, but in that religious practice it may be an act of worship.

D. Deliberately renounce each involvement on your list with a verbalized prayer like that shown below:

Lord Jesus Christ, I confess that I have been involved in the false belief of (name offense). I ask for your cleansing and forgiveness, and I renounce (offense) as a sinful counterfeit, and a sin against true Christianity. I ask my Lord Jesus Christ to reclaim all ground Satan's kingdom is claiming against me because of my involvement.

E. After working through your list with the above renunciation prayer, add this authoritative command against any
controlling, harassing powers of darness:

*In the name of my Lord Jesus Christ and by the power of His
blood, I command every wicked spirit who has assignment
against me because of my false religious practices and spiritistic
and occult sins of any kind to leave my presence. You and all your
host must go where my Lord Jesus Christ sends you.*

Step 2: Renounce All Deceptions

Step 2 is to *renounce all deception with which you are or
have been involved* (John 8:43–45; Revelation 21:8).

I. Renounce all practices of lying that have been a part of your
life.

A. Deliberate lies, half-truths, and all deceptive practices must
be honestly faced. Lying is Satan's native language and those
who resort to his ways leave themselves open for his control.

B. Ask the Lord to bring all of your lying ways to your consciousness. Since lying is a sin of the flesh, use the victory
over your flesh outlined in chapter 6 to defeat this sinful
practice.

II. Renounce those deceptive lies that you have believed and acted
upon. This is a chief area in which Christians are vulnerable in
the matter of deception. To believe a lie of the Enemy and to act
upon it is to open the door to Satan's subtle control. Examine
carefully these areas:

A. Accepting an unbiblical view of your self-worth.

B. Holding judgmental, negative views toward other believers.

C. Questioning God's love and goodness.

D. Accepting controlling fears and living them out.

III. Develop the practice of affirming and aligning yourself with the
truth in a daily pattern of discipline.

A. Memorize God's Word, the word of truth. (John 17:17)

B. Meditate on the Person of Truth, Our Lord Jesus Christ and
His finished work. Doctrinal prayer practices facilitate this
discipline. (John 14:6)

C. Meditate on the Holy Spirit's ministries. He is the Spirit of Truth. (John 14:17; 15:26; 16:13)

D. Remain loyal and an active participant in a Bible-preaching local church. It is the "pillar and foundation of truth." (1 Timothy 3:15)

IV. Renounce and claim back the ground given by the practice of lying or believing Satan's deceptions. This involves specific prayer. Here is one I recommend:

Loving Lord Jesus Christ, I recognize that I've been deceived by practicing and believing in the lying ways of Satan's native language. I specifically renounce my participation by (name lie or action) and I ask that the blood of Jesus Christ would cleanse me of this wicked insult of truth. I ask that my Lord Jesus Christ would reclaim any and all ground Satan's kingdom is claiming against me because of my participation in this lie.

V. After covering all areas of lying on your list, use an authoritative summary command of resistance. I recommend the following prayer:

In the name of my Lord Jesus Christ and by the power of His blood, I command every wicked spirit having assignment against me because of my telling lies and believing lies to leave my presence. You and all of your hosts must leave and go where the Lord Jesus Christ sends you.

Step 3: Remove Bitterness

Step 3 is to *renounce and rid yourself of all bitterness and the lack of forgiveness of others who have wounded you.*

I. Recognize that a Christian's refusal to forgive another who has wronged him is a very serious matter.

A. A lack of forgiveness gives Satan a device to take advantage of a Christian. (2 Corinthians 2:10–11)

Satan is a schemer, a manipulator, and a crafty opponent who tries to use his "devices" (2 Corinthians 2:11, NKJV) to bring believers into his control. One of his tactics seems to be to try to use God's attributes—His ways of justice and truth—to work his wicked purposes.

For example, it's plausible that Satan wants to destroy our nation. Much of God's grace has been upon our land. Satan hates the freedom that has enabled believers to send the gospel through missionary outreach to the multitudes of the world. Though he probably wants to, Satan doesn't possess the power or authority to do away with the United States of America. He cannot do that because his power to destroy is infinitely inferior to God's power to protect and bless.

To accomplish his purpose, Satan first must deceive the people of our nation to do the things that would influence God to remove His blessing and protection. That's the way he's working, and it would seem that he is dangerously close to accomplishing his evil purpose.

In 2 Corinthians 2: 10–11 the apostle Paul's indicates a lack of forgiveness is one of Satan's devices to penetrate the protection belonging to a believer.

B.   A lack of forgiveness may cause God to discipline a believer by allowing tormenting demonic activity as a corrective instrument in that believer's life. (Matthew 18:21–25, 32–35)

Jesus told the parable of the unforgiving servant (Matthew 18) to emphasize the urgency of a believer to practice forgiveness of others "seventy times seven" (v. 22, NKJV), or almost limitless times. Such enormous forgiveness reflects the level God extended toward us when He saved us. It was undeserved and unearned in any way.

In the parable, the master disciplines his unforgiving servant by turning him over to the "tormentors" (Greek *basanistees*) to suffer discipline. Who are these tormentors? The Greek word for tormentors is the same root word that Peter used to describe what happened to Lot as a result of his sojourn in Sodom (cf. 2 Peter 2:7–9). Lot's torment as a righteous man by the careless ways he was living in Sodom was the same kind that the master unleashes against his unforgiving servant. It is corrective discipline torment and not wrath torment. I strongly suspect that the tormentors are a reference to God allowing demons to harass and torment a forgiven believer who refuses to forgive. The torment is limited until the unforgiving one learns to lay aside his bitterness and forgive just as he was forgiven. Unconditionally and totally we are to forgive just as we were forgiven.

Forgiveness of others is a basic cornerstone of God's expectations of those who have been forgiven. It has nothing to do with gaining salvation, but it is a major response God expects from those who have gained salvation. A refusal to forgive stops fellowship with the Lord and circumvents blessings from Him until the issue of forgiveness is resolved. It's that important to our heavenly Father. (Within Christ's model prayer, see Matthew 6:9, 12, 14–15.)

Often all the progress of a believer in getting to know the Lord is put on hold until the believer deals with his unforgiving heart. We've found it so in spiritual warfare counseling. Sometimes it takes time to work through the brutalizing hurts of life before forgiveness is realized, but it is essential that it come. Even perverted sexual abuse by a parent or grandparent must be resolved in forgiveness before a freedom and peace comes to a wounded person. Since unforgiveness is our attempt to punish the offender, we are usurping from God what He has reserved for Himself. (See Romans 12:17–21.)

II. Recognize that forgiveness requires deliberate, willed action.

   A. Forgiveness must be based upon Christ's finished work that removes every sin from the believer's record. (Psalm 103:10–12; Colossians 2:11–15)

   B. Forgiveness must be a choice of the will; a conscious decision to let the offender off the hook and by that choice to free oneself from the past.

   C. Forgiveness must recognize the truth of your own hurt and the other person's wrong. Once recognized, you make a decision to forgive and to leave the matter totally to God.

III. Learn to practice forgiveness.

   A. Make a list of everyone who has offended or hurt you in your lifetime. Ask the Lord to help you remember each one you need to remember. You may need to include God and even yourself on your list.

B. In some cases you will profit from writing out a careful description of the nature of your hurt or feelings or hate. Be honest and express how you feel. Getting in touch with your true feelings is therapeutic. Let some tears flow if such feelings surface.

C. If possible, work through the twelve steps to forgiveness in *Victory over Darkness*, by Neil Anderson.

D. Verbalize a prayer of forgiveness and renunciation of your bitterness toward each person and incident on your list. A prayer of this kind is suggested:

Lord Jesus Christ, I've come to see that I've sinned against You and my heavenly Father by harboring resentment, hurt, and bitterness against (name of person) for his/her offense against me. Please cleanse me of this wickedness, and I now choose to forgive (name) for that wrong unconditionally and totally just as You forgave me all my sins.

E. After you've been through your list, another resistance prayer exercising your authority over intrusive demonic activity is wise. I recommend the following:

I ask my Lord Jesus Christ to reclaim all ground in my life that Satan's kingdom has claimed against me because of my unforgiving bitterness. In the name of my Lord Jesus Christ and by the power of His blood, I command all powers of darkness having assignment against me because of my unforgiving ways to leave my presence! You must go where my Lord Jesus Christ sends you. I submit my whole person and being only to the controlling and indwelling work of the Holy Spirit.

Step 4: Renounce Rebellion Against God

Step 4 is to *renounce all expressions of rebellion and your lack of submission to God's will and plan* (1 Samuel 15:22–23). Rebellion is as the sin of witchcraft in the eyes of our holy God. Samuel's reminder of this fact to Saul demonstrates the seriousness of rebellious rejection of God's directive will.

I. Ask the Lord to reveal to you all expressions of your rebellion against His authority over you.

   A. Personal spiritual attitudes of rebellion.

      1. His call upon you or His appointed place of service.

      2. All areas of willful disobedience.

      3. All areas of complaint and disappointment.

   B. Rebellion involving the rejection of God-ordained, constituted authority over you.

      1. Civil government. (Romans 13:1–5; 1 Peter 2:13–17)

      2. Parents. (Ephesians 6:1–3)

      3. Husband or wife. (Ephesians 5:25–30; 1 Peter 3:1–2)

      4. Employer. (Ephesians 6:4–9; 1 Peter 2:18–21)

      5. Church leaders. (Hebrews 13:17)

II. Specifically renounce each act of rebellion on your list. Here is a recommended prayer:

Loving heavenly Father, I confess that my sin of (name offense) is as the sin of witchcraft before Your holy eyes. I ask the Lord Jesus Christ to reclaim all ground I've given to Satan's kingdom by this rebellion and to cleanse me by His blood from all the soil of my rebellious sin. May the Holy Spirit grant to me the fruit of His submissive control over my mind, will, emotions, and body.

III. Evict any controlling spirits of rebellion with a resisting command of this nature:

In the name of my Lord Jesus Christ and by the power of His blood, I command all rebellious demonic powers seeking to rule over me because of my rebellious practices to leave my presence. You and all your hosts must go where my Lord Jesus Christ sends you.

Step 5: Recognize and Renounce Expressions of Pride

Step 5 is to *renounce all prideful expressions exalting self and claim God's grace for a humble heart.*

I. Recognize that pride was at the core of Satan's fall. (Isaiah

14:11–14; Ezekiel 28:1–19)

A. Realize that pride is our private attempt to claim to ourselves what belongs only to God. (James 4:6–10; 1 Peter 5:1–10)

B. Desire and pray for God to grant to you a humble heart. (Philippians 2:3; James 4:7–10)

C. Make a list of all the ways you see sinful pride being expressed in your life.

D. Confess and renounce sinful expressions of pride by a direct renunciation of this type:

In the name of my Lord Jesus Christ, I renounce and confess the sin of my prideful (name offense). I ask my Lord Jesus Christ to reclaim the ground this pride has given to Satan's kingdom. May the precious blood of my Lord Jesus Christ wash me clean from the soil of this sinful pride. I ask my Lord to grant to me the grace of a yielded, humble heart before Him. I here and now resist all prideful demonic attempt to rule over me in any way. In the name of my Lord Jesus Christ I command all prideful spirits and all of their host to leave me and to go where my Lord Jesus Christ sends you.

Step 6: Renounce Sins of the Flesh

Step 6 is to *renounce those besetting, fleshly sins that have in the past or are now holding you in bondage.*

I. Make a list of the besetting, fleshly sins that have or are now ruling and controlling you.

A. Go through the list of fleshly sins in Galatians 5:19–21 with prayerful honesty.

B. List those sins that have or now are controlling you, recognizing that any moral sins involving other people are uniquely significant.

1. In fornication, adultery, or homosexuality, God's plan of intimate oneness in sexual union makes the participators very vulnerable. (1 Corinthians 6:15–20; 1 Thessalonians 4:3–8)

2. The probability of demonic transfer from one person to

another in sexual oneness is very strong.

3. A listing of all partners with whom you've been sexually immoral should be confessed and renounced in prayer.[2]

II. Confess and renounce all besetting sins that have habitually ruled and controlled your life.

It is important that one apply on a moment-by-moment basis the victory over his fleshly sins. Biblical steps for applying this victory are set forth in chapters 6 and 7.

A. Recognize that a continual practice of fleshly sins gives place or ground to the Devil. (Ephesians 4:17–30)

B. Confess and renounce in a deliberate manner the ground given by habitually yielding to a besetting sin. Here is a model prayer:

I confess and renounce my repeated yielding to my besetting sin of (name the sin) as an act that gives ground or place for the rule of unclean spirits in my life. I ask that the blood of my Lord Jesus Christ would wash me clean from the soil and power of this besetting sin. I ask that my Lord Jesus Christ would reclaim all the ground that I've given by this often-repeated sin. In the name of my Lord Jesus Christ and by the power of His blood, I command the unclean spirit of (name besetting sin) and all of his host to leave my presence. You must now go where my Lord Jesus Christ sends you.

Step 7: Renounce the Claims of Darkness from Generational Transfer

Step 7 is to *renounce the claims of darkness focused against you because of the sins of those in your ancestral lineage.* Such generational claims can give significant ground to Satan's kingdom by their sinful practices. (cf. Exodus 20:4–6 with 1 Peter 1:13–21)

I. Recognize that generational transfer claim by the powers of darkness remains somewhat controversial. (see pages 51–53, Chapter 2)

A. Study carefully the biblical passages in this book dealing with generational transfer.

    B. Realize that the demonic influence from personal actions is always more significant than that from generational choices.

II. Handle generational transfer claims with responsible, prayerful care.

    A. It helps explain demonic activity in the lives of little children. (Mark 9:14–29)

    B. Generational claim provides insight into the "third and fourth" generational consequences of the sins of the fathers. (Exodus 20:4–5)

    C. The experiences of warfare counselors bear extensive witness that the powers of darkness frequently express generational claim.

III. Renounce generational or ancestral claim on the basis of Christ's atoning blood. (1 Peter 1:13–21)

    A. A deliberate renouncing of all generational claim needs prayerful and tactful research. Sometimes one can do this by simply observing the obvious defeats that were visible in our parents' and grandparents' lives. Conversations with living family members may also reveal suspected strongholds that were visible in the lives of our family lineage. Again it is helpful to make a list of those things that may give suggestion or hint of strongholds that existed in our generational lineage. Do it for each side of your parental heritage. Make a list for your mother's side of the family and another for your father's side of the family.

        The listing may include practices or behavioral traits that range from occult practices to alcoholism and gambling addictions. They may also include emotional responses and practices.[3]

    B. As a deliberate renouncing of all generational claim, it would be good to include the naming of specific areas where there seems evidence of possible generational strongholds. A biblical renunciation pattern might be phrased in this manner:

Through the power of the precious blood of my Lord Jesus Christ. I affirm that I have been redeemed from all consequences of the empty way of life handed down to me and my family through the sins and failures of my forefathers on my father's side of the family. I specifically renounce strongholds of: (name those recognized as possible areas where much ground has been given. Name them by being as extensive and specific as you feel you need to be). In the name of my Lord Jesus Christ, I forbid any powers of darkness to try to control me or the family members for whom I am responsible because of ground given by my father's generational lineage extending back three and four generations. I renounce such claim. I affirm and claim the death, burial, and resurrection of my Lord Jesus Christ to be fully sufficient to release me and set me and my family totally free from all generational transfer claim of the powers of darkness.

After dealing with any generational claim by the powers against your father's side of the family, exercise the same care to deal with your generational heritage on your mother's side of the family. Stepparents and adoptive parents should also be included in most cases.

C. When those in our immediate family lineage are living a lifestyle that gives ground to the Enemy, a continuing renunciation of transfer claim should be affirmed. Grandparents, parents, brothers or sisters, and even uncles or aunts need to be considered in this light. Occult activity is of special significance. A prayer similar to that in point B would be appropriate.

D. The above renunciations have great importance for use by the parents of adopted children. Bloodline siblings, parents, grandparents, and others may be giving ground to the work of Satan's kingdom. As adoptive parents, they have responsibility and spiritual authority to exercise protective care over their children.

THE POWER OF RENUNCIATION PRAYING

When one has worked through the steps to freedom, a prayerful time of waiting before the Lord is desirable and often very beneficial. The sincere confessions, renunciations, and assertions of the believer's authority over darkness will both strengthen the believer and weaken the assaulting powers of darkness. For many the release and freedom will be readily self-evident and immediate.

"I've never felt so clean and free," stated a medical doctor upon having worked through the steps. "I only wish I would have been helped to go through these steps years ago."

A college student gave a similar statement about her final year of school compared to her junior year. After going through what's been outlined in this chapter, her release was dramatic. "I never realized I was under so much stress and bondage from the Evil One. I had put all the blame on myself, but now that I'm free I can see how deceived I was."

A businessman who had difficulty working through the renunciation of besetting sins because of a past promiscuous lifestyle, found a marvelous renewal in his marriage and family relationship. As he had renounced the bonding of his past sexual sins, fierce opposition came against him in confused thoughts and spiritual oppression. We had to stop several times and command the interference to release him and be subdued. "I see my relationship to my wife in an entirely new frame of reference. I would never have believed that something as basic as the freedom steps could transform our marriage so totally," he declared after some months had passed.

With a joyful smile his wife confirmed his remarks. "I not only have back the husband I married," she told me, "but he is more thoughtful, considerate, and supportive than I ever dreamed he could be."

One wishes that everyone going through the steps would experience such dramatic change. That hasn't been so, but I do believe everyone I have led through the steps has received marked benefit. These steps have been a significant step toward claiming their freedom. At some time in the counseling process, I try to take each counselee through these important steps. In some cases after a time lapse and when needed, I've helped them through more than one application of their steps to freedom.

In my limited counseling exposure to them, even those recovering from satanic ritual abuse, multiple personality disorder (MPD) and Dissociative Identity Disorder (DID) have experienced benefit and renewed encouragement from working through the steps.

After completing the steps as outlined above, I have the counselee read through a wrap-up prayer. The prayer can be used anytime one senses the need to use it. It's a tool to yield one's self to the sanctifying work of grace that the Holy Spirit is ready and able to do in each believer. The prayer is reproduced in Appendix 4, "A Model Prayer for Continuing Resistance to Demonic Influence." Readers should feel free to copy it and keep it convenient for use. Whether you are a college student with an infant son or a businessman with a teenage daughter does not matter. If you sense you need spiritual freedom in your life, strongly consider following the seven steps to freedom described in this chapter. You will benefit and your children will too, as you find strength to help them grow to confront one day the wolves of this world.

CHAPTER ELEVEN

PRAYER THAT DEFEATS THE RULE OF EVIL

Sally Graham, a supervisor in a Midwest manufacturing plant, has lived in America's heartland for almost twenty-five years. More important, she has become a veteran at warfare praying for herself and her children. Each of her three children has benefited from her watchful prayers even prior to being born. For the benefit of other parents who are just learning about warfare praying, I asked Sally to describe some of her experiences gleaned from many years of prayerful watch.

At this writing, her two sons, Kevin and Steve, are ages ten and sixteen, respectively. Kelly, her only daughter, is nineteen. Sally has lifted from each child's life an incident of warfare that significantly made a difference. Except for editing changes, the accounts are her written remembrances, used by permission.

The three accounts will touch your heart with one mother's candor and openness about her own failures and flaws. Her wisdom, vulnerability, compassionate understanding, and close identification with each child shout a message. Parenting demands spiritual insights and consistent application of spiritual principles. Sally has both. Reading these three accounts reminds us that as parents we face battles in rearing our children among a world of wolves.

THE GRAHAMS' SPIRITUAL BATTLES

Kevin's Story

"Mommy, every time you turn out the light and leave my room, I see a face on my ceiling!" Kevin was clutching my hand and whispering to me. His frightened, intense voice was at a level just above a whisper. I knew my seven-year-old was really spooked. He was afraid! The sinister appearing face on the ceiling with its threatening sneer had unnerved my youngest child. As he told me, I felt a familiar chill I had experienced before when spirit powers were lurking about. They are very real and they want us to be afraid.

I considered myself a spiritual warfare veteran. I'd experienced twenty-five years of exercising daily, active, warfare praying over my own life and the lives of friends and family members. Kevin was my third child and although this was the first experience with a "face" appearance, we'd weathered several other encounters with supernatural evil. I knew how to deal with a matter like this. I was mindful to reassure Kevin by my measured calm that he didn't have to be afraid.

"Kevin, we can take care of that problem right now!" I assured my son. "The face you see is there because Satan's kingdom wants to rule you by fear. But we have the Lord Jesus Christ on our side and we can make this stop." I took him into my arms. He was quieted by my approach and greatly reassured that his Lord was in charge. I then began to pray aloud with bold confidence:

In the name of the Lord Jesus Christ and by the power of His blood, I bind away all workings of Satan or any of his kingdom who are putting faces on the ceiling to frighten Kevin. I command these wicked powers to leave our house, our family, and Kevin's mind and room. You must go to the place the Lord Jesus

Christ sends you. As a Christian united with my Lord Jesus Christ, as a priest of the living and true God and as Kevin's protecting mother, I forbid these wicked powers to work in our home again in any way. I ask our heavenly Father to station His holy angels in Kevin's room to insure the end of these evil intrusions.

As I finished my prayer, Kevin hugged me appreciatively. I returned his hug and gave him a mother's loving kiss. "You don't have to be afraid, Kevin. Mommy's not afraid of any old faces the Devil tries to use to scare us. If that ever happens again, you command it to leave with a prayer like this: 'In the name of the Lord Jesus Christ, leave my room right now!' If they don't leave immediately, then you come and get me and I'll pray again so you can go back to sleep."

Though he nodded his agreement, I could sense Kevin's apprehension over those ending words. He wasn't interested in having to handle any more encounters with faces. His confidence was building, however, and he did need to resist on his own. His dad and I prayed over his room with him before the lights were turned off, but even then the apparitions tried to return. Kevin began to resist with his own heart and authority. The faces disappeared and have never returned.

My husband Charlie and I were reared in a generation of Christian parents and grandparents who did not understand spiritual warfare. Charlie had seen apparitions in the form of snakes on his bedroom walls when he was a child. He cried about it and complained several times to his parents. Because of a lack of training and biblical perspective, his parents didn't hold a clue to what was happening to Charlie. They used the rational, logical approach: "Charlie, there are absolutely no snakes on the walls of your room! Now you just forget about such nonsense!"

Of course, Charlie's parents were right. Real snakes were not crawling on Charlie's walls. Nevertheless, Charlie was seeing something very real. Not recognizing the battle and failing to use the available tools to make the apparitions cease not only harmed my husband but had left the door open for the harassment of our son. That's a spiritual tragedy.

I praise the Lord that He is opening the eyes of many Christian parents in this generation. He is opening our eyes not only to the reality of physical and spiritual opposition from spirit beings, but He is also showing us His power to stop these attacks. Charlie's parents have also come to understand warfare and join us in praying for their grandchildren. That's brought an added power dimension.

Three years after I prayed on Kevin's behalf, my youngest child said to one of his grandparents, "I just couldn't live a single day without my Lord! He helps me in everything I have to do!" He's all boy, but he is growing to love and appreciate how necessary and powerful is his Lord. That's the greatest lesson he will ever learn.

If you suspect that your child may be experiencing some attack from darkness, don't let that frighten you or send you down "denial road." Don't let yourself be caught up in a forest of "why trees." (Why, God, is this happening to such a small, innocent child? Why can the enemy still work on my son when we're a Christian family and have dedicated ourselves to you?) That's such a sinkhole. It's a death trap of doubt trying to rule. God's answer is simply to use boldly the tools and weapons of warfare made so available to us. We will then see the attacks ceasing and the reality of our faith being lived out in the crucible of victorious spiritual conflict. Like Kevin, we all have to learn: "I just couldn't live a single day without my Lord!"

Steve's Story

There had been a special closeness between my older son, Steve, and me until he reached his twelfth year. I felt the pain of that normal growing-up process where a son often withdraws from Mom. I'd observed most of the boys I've known go through difficult behavior patterns as they progressed through puberty. For that reason, I was not too threatened by his turning away from Mom. He was merely "cutting the apron strings" in keeping with the hormonal changes necessary for his manhood. Though it hurt to see my little boy growing up, I took it all pretty much in stride.

As we entered the second year of "normal adolescent resistance and irritability," I noted a subtle shift in Steve's attitudes toward me. What I had accepted as an immature lack of tolerance and impatient annoyance now included fierce anger and even emotions of hatred. Instead of simply challenging my views with his own contrary thinking, Steve began to taunt me and ridicule my opinions. When he was around me, he set himself up as the final authority on every issue. I knew we had moved from a normal growth pattern to a danger zone of rebellion. A worrisome concern settled in on me.

I didn't handle Steve's growing challenge to my parental authority at all well. I was being "sucked under" emotionally. The verbal badgering, the scornful looks, and the lack of respect were extremely threatening to me. I was feeling considerable anger. I was not about to let my son rule me or run his own life at thirteen years of age. My whole perspective of biblical principles caused me to justify my responses to my son's challenge. I handled the problem very badly.

I began to fight the battle with lectures and shouting. Every time Steve would "write me off" or "shut me out" I would go into a slow burn. I began to "cook" emotionally. The pressure cooker was really building up steam. Finally the pot boiled over. Steve and I fell into a screaming, shouting, and shoving encounter that left us both exhausted and weeping. A depressed sense of parental failure was now added to my resentment and anger.

The explosive trauma did stop me in my destructive responses to a very needy problem. I began to see spiritual truth again. . . . Though I thought of myself as a "warfare mom," I had to admit that I had not seen this battle from a spiritual perspective. My pastor counselor helped both Steve and me regain some perspective. We needed to fight the right enemy and use weapons of warfare to help us properly relate.

As soon as I could get alone, I drew apart into my Lord's presence. After some sweet repentance time, I sensed the need for warfare prayer against what the Enemy was doing to the relationship between Steve and me. With tearful, but now righteous, anger, I was able to pray aggressively:

In the name of the Lord Jesus Christ and by the power of His blood, I pull down the walls, relationships, and barriers that Satan and his kingdom are building between Steve and me. I ask the Lord Jesus Christ to demolish all of the destructive strongholds that the kingdom of darkness has been able to erect between us. I ask my Lord to unleash the mighty power of the loving heavenly Father upon our relationship to make it all that You want it to be. I ask the Holy Spirit to put within me and Steve God's fruit of love, joy, peace, patience, kindness, goodness, faithfulness, gentleness, and self-control. By faith, I pray the healing power of the true and living God upon our broken relationship that we might glorify Your name.

In that quiet time alone with the Lord, I also prayed for wisdom to know how to reach my son. I knew my resentful anger had deeply wounded him. I felt so ashamed. Satan even wanted to use my guilt to stop my move toward victory, but I would have none of that. The Lord began to give me immediate insights. I needed to apologize and ask Steve's forgiveness for my wrong responses to his evident needs. He also gave me insights about verbalizing my admiration for Steve and the talents God had put into him. He needed the ministry of his mom's encouragement now more than ever.

The Lord also showed me that in my hurt toward Steve, I had abandoned all physical gestures toward my son that communicate caring love. I knew I had to be more mature now and not treat him as a little boy, but physical gestures that communicate love were desperately important to rebuild the brokenness between us. At first it was difficult. Even a hand on the shoulder elicited stiff, rigid body language. I was not deterred. I ignored his unreturned hugs. By faith I kept reaching out to him with physical gestures. A light tap on the shoulder as I commended some aspect of his growing manhood, a squeeze of his arm, even an occasional tousling of his hair began to communicate. The hugs and quick kisses as we parted were a part of God's rebuilding tools. One day I saw a flickering smile of appreciation on his face; that was the beginning of Steve's ability to return my gestures with hugs of his own. We were on our way.

Verbal commendations and physical gestures of caring love were very important to the healing of our broken relationship. Within a week, the tensions were fading. Within the first month, I was confident that we were out of the danger zone. Warfare praying began to destroy the spiritual walls of hostility and hatred that darkness had been building. I intensified my intercessions.

We've come a long way since those dark days of defeat. I feel we have reached a better than "normal" relationship. Now sixteen and six feet tall, Steve has a deep bass voice. His fully developed, adult body has moved beyond much of the "hormonal craziness" we once faced. He's becoming a godly man. I'm so thankful! Grace really is unmerited favor and is working even when we tragically "blow it." I know warfare prayer made the difference. Without the use of those "weapons of warfare" the Lord Jesus Christ won for us on the cross and in His resurrection, I'm certain . . . our relationship would have still been in crisis and getting worse by the day. Disaster would have overtaken us. Thank You, Lord Jesus Christ, for Your rescue!

Kelly's Story

From my biased perspective, Kelly has been the perfect daughter from the day she was born. I called her my "warfare baby." As she lay in her crib each night, I would stand there in the shadows of her room and pray the Ephesians 6 spiritual armor on her. I often think in picture format, and I could visualize each tiny piece of specially designed baby armor fitting into place on her little person:

> In the name of the Lord Jesus Christ and by the power of His blood, I put the full armor of God upon Kelly Christian Graham. I place on her the belt of truth, the breastplate of righteousness, the sandals of peace, the shield of faith, the helmet of salvation, and the sword of the Spirit. I place upon her and all around her the covering of the precious blood of the Lord Jesus Christ and the protection of prayer. I ask my heavenly Father to assign holy angels to watch over her and protect her. I invite the Holy Spirit to minister to every part of her being. Bring her to Christ when she's old enough to understand and fill her with love, joy, peace,

patience, kindness, goodness, faithfulness, gentleness, and self-control from infancy on. I ask You, dear heavenly Father, to make Kelly everything You desire her to be.

If I could relate to you how wonderfully the Lord answered those prayers, you would find it difficult to believe. Though she gave evidence of the fallen nature we all receive from our first parents, to me she was a dream child come true. Now nineteen, she's in her second year at a Christian college, where she has enjoyed dating several young men. This is important because her dating life in high school was so bleak it was almost nonexistent. I'm sorry to have to admit again that her "warfare mom" did not recognize the spiritual nature of her dateless life until some severe emotional damage had occurred to Kelly.

Kelly had many friends in both school and church. Her personality, long blond hair, and hourglass figure enabled her to be chosen as a cheerleader. Yet, unbelievable as it sounds, she had never been asked out for a date. At first, she laughed it off, but eventually it got to her.

As her junior year began, Kelly decided at the urging of one of her best friends to stop feeling sorry for herself about her dateless life. She should take matters into her own hands and ask one of her Christian male friends to take her to homecoming. It would just be a friendship night out where she could at least get in on some of the social fun.

Kelly first called Tom. She'd enjoyed several study times with Tom when he'd come over to the house for the evening. Tom turned her down cold. The worst was that he apparently concluded that Kelly had a crush on him and he changed his whole attitude toward her. He avoided her. He wouldn't speak to her or even look her way for several months.

She asked Jim next. They had been good friends since the fifth grade. Though not attracted to him in any romantic way, she liked his sense of humor and quiet friendliness. Jim, too, said no without any explanation. Their friendly relationship also seemed to be fractured after that.

Kelly was shattered. The humiliation of asking and being

refused was almost unbearable. "What is wrong with me? Why do boys hate me?" Her hurtful wail almost broke my heart. Yet, I didn't know what to say. . . .

As girlfriend after girlfriend went on date after date, Kelly began to withdraw. I gave my speeches about trusting God with your life. In a desperate attempt to be helpful, I mumbled out one day, "Maybe God wants you to be single, honey. You have to be open to His perfect will for your life." That was a real zinger. My pious platitude only added to Kelly's dirge of despair. She was hurt, disappointed, and hopelessly empty. What aroused my righteous anger was the lie I could see building in Kelly's mind and emotions. She was seeing herself as ugly and undesirable to anyone. A false perception of her true worth was pressing in on her because of her dating circumstances.

When Kelly was just a small child, Charlie and I had decided that we would only allow her to date Christians when she was old enough for that social life. When we explained that to her as she reached the dating age, Kelly accepted the restriction without question. She saw the biblical principle of warning against an unequal yoke and was glad for the guidance of her parents. The large youth program of our church provided many opportunities for social interaction with Christian young men. Now this Christian mom couldn't understand what went wrong. Were these Christian fellows blind or what?

As Kelly began her senior year, I wondered if she would face another dateless year. I finally began to feel some spiritual concern. As I saw the deep wounding she was experiencing over this issue, I decided to lay it before the Lord. I was concerned about her deepening depression, and I could do nothing to help her with my words and advice. I also felt that she had patiently waited long enough. If it was God's plan for Kelly to remain single, that was completely acceptable to me, but Kelly needed spiritual help. She needed to be rid of her "I'm a reject" self-image. It was building destructive patterns into her life that caused me deep concern.

I decided to fast and pray over Kelly's dating life for three days. As I started into the second day of the fast, I was feeling less than enthusiastic and besides that I was extremely hungry.

Kelly had snapped out of the depression and seemed resigned to the fact that she would not have a date to homecoming again this year. I was about to break my fast but thought it best to seek the Lord's approval before making such a decision. I started to pray: "Lord, You know I am very hungry. Please let me break this fast now if it isn't accomplishing Your will. I'm not only hungry but I'm not even sure of the purpose of my fast. Please give me guidance now in a way that will confirm Your will to me."

Immediately, my mind seemed activated. I saw a strong, formidable-looking wall in my mind picture. Large, ugly, evil, sinister-looking soldiers were standing shoulder to shoulder guarding the wall. I saw the mind picture as God's insight into what was happening in Kelly's dating life. The Enemy had built strongholds of opposition and isolation around her. He was using it to destroy her sense of self-worth and ultimately to destroy her.

My devotional reading through the One-Year Bible for that day had a message of confirmation about my mind picture. I could scarcely believe it as I read: "Let my eyes overflow with tears night and day without ceasing; for my virgin daughter . . . has suffered a grievous wound, a crushing blow" (Jeremiah 14:17). I wept and thanked God for His personalized message in the midst of my frustration and need.

I continued my fast and prayer "without ceasing" for the remaining days of my commitment. I feel the Lord let me see a clear picture of the "crushing blow" in Kelly's life and the reason for it. It was a vicious attack from the realm of darkness. I had prayed over Kelly and her future husband from the day she was born, but I had never covered her dating life with warfare prayer. Strongholds had been able to build with their evil purposes, in part because of my failure in watchfulness.

After completing the fast, I felt I needed to share with Kelly my new insights about the battle. She had a good understanding of balanced spiritual warfare and I knew she'd respond well. "Kelly, I've been unaware and insensitive to the level of pain and loss you've been experiencing over this dating issue. Though I haven't completely understood, God has. He knows exactly how you feel and He hurts with you." I went on to share the story of my fast, the mind picture and the Bible reading text which proved how much God knew and cared.

As I began to read the verses, Kelly buried her face in her pillow and began to weep. When she was able to compose herself, we read together *Warfare Prayer* by Victor Matthew. As we finished, Kelly breathed a deep sigh of relief and slipped quickly into a restful sleep. Her nap was short. Fifteen minutes later, the phone rang. It was for Kelly. A young man was calling to ask her to be his date to homecoming. She accepted!

My purpose in sharing this very personal account from our daughter's life is not to say that all dateless lives are caused by problems with the kingdom of darkness. Your daughter's problem might be that every boy around seems to want to date her. The issue is a watchful awareness that the destroying tactics of darkness over our children are subtle and ingenious. If you are a follower of the Lord Jesus Christ and you have given to Him the control of your life and the ownership of your children, you have powerful weapons to use in their defense. You can wage a winning war against the darkness seeking to rule them. Use your weapons!

WARFARE PRAYERS TO PROTECT YOUR CHILDREN

Building on Sally Graham's testimony, I want to bring together a number of doctrinal warfare prayers to provide patterns of prayer that parents and grandparents may find helpful. Some of the prayers are new and some of them have appeared in my previous writings. Many have found these written, doctrinal prayers extremely helpful in teaching them how to use their authority in Christ to resist the works of darkness.

A Prayer for the Parent

Praying these prayers should take place in an atmosphere of confidence, not fear. If a parent communicates terror as he prays for his children, the parent neither reassures the child nor has effective faith in God. Yet I know many Christian parents whose prayers are undermined because of their own fears for their child's safety. Therefore, before praying for your child, it would be wise to pray for yourself as a parent. Here is a sample prayer to combat fear of a loss of a child by injury, illness, or violence.[1]

Loving God and Father of our Lord Jesus Christ, I deliberately yield up _____ into Your loving hands of care and protection. I hold the victory and name of the Lord Jesus Christ over _____ as protection against the plans of darkness to harm and destroy _____. I ask You to assign holy angel protection and the sealing ministry of the Holy Spirit upon _____ at all times. I recognize the Enemy's effort to put a spirit of fear and terror upon me of losing _____. I thank You for the love You have given to me for him/her, but I reject the fearful unbelief that darkness is trying to use to control me. Although I trust that I will never have to face the loss of _____, I know that You would supply me with the portion of grace and mercy I would need to walk with You through such a trial. Again, I deliberately yield up my children, myself, and all of our family into the care and keeping power of the true and living God.

We need to stress again that the following prayers must not be used with the thought that they have special magical powers associated with them. Such usage or even the thought of it would be an abomination before God. It is only the eternal truth of God and the doctrinal verities of the Christian faith that force darkness to retreat. Please use them with that awareness in mind. Expressing the same truth in terminology more familiar to yourself will be just as effective as the use of my suggested wording.

Protection for Children as They Go to Sleep at Night

In the name of the Lord Jesus Christ, I commit _____'s mind, will, emotions, and body into the keeping, protecting power of the Lord Jesus Christ and the sealing ministry of the Holy Spirit while he/she sleeps. I bind and forbid any powers of darkness to tamper with any part of _____'s person on the conscious, subconscious,

or unconscious level. Heavenly Father, assign Your protecting, holy angels to watch over _____'s person and room to insure that no powers of darkness may intrude in any way while _____ sleeps.

Hostility and Quarreling Between Children

Lord Jesus Christ, I know that fleshly sinfulness can be very contentious as You have taught us in Your Word. Help me teach to my children the biblical principles of overcoming their flesh. I do note levels of hostility and fighting that could well indicate spirit powers of darkness seeking to control _____ and _____. I pull down all intensifying influences of darkness that are building walls, barriers, and hostile relationships between my children. In the name of my Lord Jesus Christ, I forbid any powers of darkness to create contention, anger, hate, and fighting between my children. I ask that the lordship of Jesus Christ and the ministry of the Holy Spirit would create the loving relationships within our family that honor You and bless our family.

Interest in Violence and Cruelty

In the name of my Lord Jesus Christ, I stand against the violence and cruelty being fostered in our culture through the entertainment media. I recognize the cultural focus on violence as an expression of the murderous ways of Satan's darkness. Loving heavenly Father, I bring to You my concern for the tendency towards violence and cruelty that I see in my child, _____. In the name of my Lord Jesus Christ and by the power of His blood, I resist and renounce all powers of darkness seeking to rule and control _____. I stand against them and command them to leave _____ and they must go where the Lord Jesus Christ commands them to go. I ask that the Holy Spirit would establish the loving gentleness of Christ in _____'s life.

Hostility to the Spiritual Things of God

Heavenly Father, I know that Satan and his kingdom stand in arrogant opposition to You and all of Your ways of righteousness and truth. When I note hostile attitudes toward the things of God in _____'s life, I know that he/she is being deceived by the kingdom of darkness. I stand against the control and deception in the name

of the Lord Jesus Christ. I renounce and tear down those strong-holds of darkness promoting hostility to spiritual truth in ____'s life. I ask You to evict them from ____'s presence. I look to You, heavenly Father, to soften ____'s heart by the work of Your Spirit and to draw ____ to Yourself.

Unwholesome Relationships

You have told us in Your Word, heavenly Father, that "Bad compa-ny corrupts good character." Because of that truth, I have deep concern for the corrupting influence I see ____ having on ____. In the name of my Lord Jesus Christ, I pull down all relationships between ____ and ____ that are being promoted and strategized by the kingdom of darkness. I ask the Lord Jesus Christ to sever all of the unwholesome bonding that is taking place between ____ and ____. I ask that You would sovereignly bring into ____'s life only those wholesome relationships that are Your direct answer for ____'s spiritual development and moral integrity.

Occult "Gifts" and Spiritistic Interests

Heavenly Father, I thank You for the direct warnings in Your Word against all occult and spiritistic activities. We have sought to care-fully warn and protect our children against any interests in such evil things of darkness. I do note in ____'s life a magnetic fascina-tion with the spiritistic realm, especially as it relates to (name it: i.e., clairvoyance, fortune-telling, Ouija boards, levitation, etc.). I stand against all powers of darkness seeking to influence and draw ____ into these spiritistic interests. I resist them in the name of the Lord Jesus Christ and command them to cease their wicked influence, and they must leave ____ and go where the Lord Jesus Christ sends them.

Preoccupation with the Opposite Sex

Thank You, heavenly Father, that You have a choice life partner in Your holy plan for ____'s life. I have prayed for You to keep ____ for that chosen one and keep him/her for ____. Thank You for hearing my prayer and I look to You to sovereignly work it out in your perfect time and way. I pray against the unwholesome attrac-tion toward the opposite sex that I see developing in ____'s life. I *stand against any corrupting schemes of darkness that may be promoting this preoccupation with the opposite sex in ____'s life. In the name of my Lord Jesus Christ, I resist their evil work and command them to leave ____ and go where the Lord Jesus sends them. I ask for wisdom and understanding of how to help ____ develop spiritually sensitive attitudes toward the opposite sex that will honor and glorify God.*

Rebellion Against Authority

In the name of the Lord Jesus Christ and by the power of His blood, I come against the spirit of rebellion that I see seeking to deceive and control ____. I renounce and resist that spirit of rebellion and all of his hosts that are influencing ____ to reject authority. I command you and your hosts to leave ____, and you must go where the Lord Jesus Christ sends you. I ask that the Holy Spirit would effect within ____'s person the same submissive attitude toward authority that the Lord Jesus Christ demonstrated in His earthly life.

Sexual Perversion Tendencies

Loving heavenly Father, I thank You for Your high and holy purpose for human sexuality. I pray the name of my Lord Jesus Christ against the pervertedness and misuse of this God-given gift that is so common to our culture. Through my words, prayers, and conduct, grant me the wisdom to convey to my children biblical values concerning their sexuality. In the name of my Lord Jesus Christ and by the power of His blood, I resist all strongholds of sexual pervertedness assigned to manipulate and rule over ____'s sexuality. I specifically resist strongholds of ____ (name any perverted sexual tendency observed in your child; i.e., pornography, masturbation, same-sex attraction, etc.). I command them to cease all activity against ____. They and all their hosts must leave ____ and go where the Lord Jesus Christ sends them.

Drugs and Other Intoxicants

In the name of my Lord Jesus Christ and by the power of His blood, I come against those manipulating powers of darkness seeking to create and intensify ____'s dependence upon ____ (name intoxi-

cant) to cope with life. I renounce and reject that deception of darkness in ____'s life that has made him/her dependent upon this counterfeit bondage. I ask the lord Jesus Christ to evict all powers of darkness associated with ____'s bondage to the place where they can never control or manipulate him/her again. I look to the shepherding lordship of Jesus Christ to effect the release and freedom of ____. May the mighty work of the Holy Spirit remove this counterfeit dependence and replace it with the joyful fruit of His full control.

Spiritistic Bombardment in Entertainment, Education, Etc.

Loving heavenly Father, I know that You hate our culture's preoccupation with spiritistic themes and all that promotes supernatural evil. I cry out against it in prayer and ask You to bring this practice into discredit and rejection in our culture. Grant to me the wisdom and action to be salt and light against this darkness. Help me to warn and inform my children about the evils of these bombardments from many sources. In the name of the Lord Jesus Christ I ask for You to protect them from any harm from these influences of darkness. Grant them the wisdom to discern and reject spiritistic promotion and activity whenever they are confronted with it.

Lack of Purpose and Goals for the Future

Thank You, heavenly Father, that "All the days ordained for ____ were written in Your book before one of them came to be" (Psalm 139:16). I rejoice in Your good and satisfying plan for ____'s future. At the present moment, the sense of direction and life purpose for ____ seems hidden from him/her. In the name of the Lord Jesus Christ, I resist all efforts of darkness to obscure and misdirect ____'s life into a purposeless future. I ask for You to sovereignly direct and reveal to ____ Your appointed plan for (him/her). Grant to ____ the wisdom to discern that plan and to enter into it in obedience to Your will.

For a Child in an Out-of-Control Behavior Pattern

Parental wisdom and judgment are needed here. Sometimes it may be wiser to slip away to a private place for this intercession. At other times it may be important to take your distraught little child into your arms and pray for him in his hearing. The size of your child, the nature of the loss of control, the place and time, and the past history of the out-of-control problem are factors that will influence your application of prayer.

> *In the mighty name of my Lord Jesus Christ and by the power of His blood, I come against any and all powers of darkness causing or intensifying the out-of-control behavior of _____. I subdue you and all your workers in the presence of the Lord Jesus Christ and I command you to cease your wicked, manipulative work against _____. You and all your host must leave _____'s presence, and you must go where the Lord Jesus Christ sends you. I ask You, Lord Jesus Christ, to bring _____ into the self-control that is authored by the Holy Spirit according to Your will and plan for _____'s life.*

For a Child Hearing Voices, Etc.

At times a child may hear voices, or report seeing images (apparitions) in the room. These may be more than just dreams or a vivid imagination at work. The child may be experiencing visits with spirit powers. He or she may even report having a conversation with someone in the room, even though no one is there. Here is a prayer for a child hearing voices, seeing apparitions, or having visits or conversations with spirit powers.

> *In the name of the Lord Jesus Christ and by the power of His blood, I bind away and command to cease all wicked spirit activity seeking to approach and communicate with _____. I ask You, Lord Jesus Christ, to order these intrusive powers away from _____'s presence and that You would confine them where they may never frighten or come near to _____ again. I ask You, heavenly Father, to provide Your protecting, holy angels to guard and secure the safety of _____. May those evil plans of darkness to control _____ through fear and deception be exposed by Your words of truth and destroyed by Your provisions of grace.*

Children's Phobias

Children have many fears growing up in a chaotic world. Some of those fears are natural and pass with time, such as fear of the dark or being left alone at home. But others can be more pervasive and capture the child in turmoil and fright. Often those sinister fears come from the powers of darkness trying to dominate the child. Here is a prayer to use when your child feels overwhelmed, even oppressed, by a particular fear.

> *In the name of my Lord Jesus Christ, I renounce and resist all powers of darkness trying to rule over _____ by producing fear and terror of _____ (name the kind of fear being observed; i.e., snakes, illness, closed places, death of parent, etc.). In my union with the Lord Jesus Christ, I command all strongholds of fear and all of their host to leave _____, and you must go where the Lord Jesus Christ sends you. I ask that the Holy Spirit would replace the rule of fear with the love and peace and all the fruit of His control in _____'s life.*

Similarly, children can pray to overcome their fears. Children who know the Lord Jesus Christ as Savior need to be taught to resist the Enemy. They can begin praying at any age when they are old enough to understand the issue and are trusting God. Some children can learn to resist as young as age four or five. Others might need to be eight or nine before they would comprehend and be ready. Maturity is the issue, not specific age. The following pattern may be helpful to train them to resist.

> *In the name of my Lord Jesus Christ and by the blood He shed on the cross, I stand against all powers of darkness trying to make me fearful of _____. I resist you and I command all powers of fear troubling me to go where the Lord Jesus Christ sends you. I ask the Lord Jesus Christ to comfort me and to put His courage within my heart.*

Transfer to Adopted Children

In chapter 2, we discussed how a delayed harvest can affect your children if they are adopted. Even if you have no contact with the biological parents, you can help your adopted children resist generational transfer by using a prayer such as the following. Note that there is a place to sign after praying.

You may want to copy the prayer and sign it, as a reminder of your commitment to the specific adopted child and to God to guard this child's welfare as he/she remains under your care.

> *In the name of the Lord Jesus Christ, I praise my heavenly Father that He has entrusted to me my adopted child, _____. I accept all responsibility that God places upon me to be a godly, protecting parent in _____'s life. In keeping with the legal adoption in the laws of our state, I ask my heavenly Father to sever all spiritual and generational claim to _____ from the bloodline parentage that would bring any harmful influences into _____'s life and future. I ask that all generational virtues or blessings that would normally pass on to _____ from the generational bloodline be retained for _____'s future benefit and spiritual blessing. I ask that the spiritual, protective, and parental rights and responsibilities for _____ be fully bestowed upon us as the adoptive parents.*
>
> *I ask You, Lord Jesus Christ, through the power of Your name and finished work to sever all claims of darkness against _____ because of generational curses, occult rituals, or satanic covenants entered into by bloodline ancestors of _____. I look to the sovereign lordship and shepherding care of the Lord Jesus Christ to bring _____ to eternal salvation and God's gracious will and plan in _____'s life. I will only accept in my adopted child's life that which comes by way of the cross and in keeping with the grace and will of the true and living God.*
>
> *(Sign with name and date.)*

Protection from "Child Snatching" or Sexual Abuse by Others

In these evil days, each child deserves this kind of protective prayer cover as a regular practice. Psalm 91 is there for parents to claim. Memorize it and daily pray its truth over your family. Here is one prayer of protection.

> *Heavenly Father, we live in a very wicked world! Only You know the awful depth of the evil and wickedness that is before You. One of the worst expressions of this evil is the brutal harm done to little children by sinful people. Often it ends in sexual abuse and even the violent death of the child. Thank You for Your hatred of this*

despicable evil. You warned such an abuser that, "It would be bet-
ter for him to be thrown into the sea with a large millstone tied
around his neck" (Mark 9:42). Thank You for Your holy wrath. I
ask You to stand with me, and for me, to insure Your watchful
protection against any such evils happening to _____. I have made
You my dwelling and I depend upon You to assign Your holy
angels in constant protective care of _____.

May the most clever ploy of Satan and the wicked people he con-
trols be unable to touch _____ in any way. Grant to me the wisdom
to be alert and watchful, but only Your sovereign, ever-present
awareness is sufficient protection from this evil.

Different Harmful Behavior Patterns

Here is a model prayer for any of several harmful behavior patterns, such as pouting, manipulative efforts; swearing,
cursing; stealing and theft. The following prayer pattern can
also be used when a parent detects frequent critical, negative
attitudes, pride, arrogance, greed, or materialism.

Heavenly Father, I see the influence of the world and the fleshly
desires of _____ creating a pattern of _____ (name the problem
area) within _____'s life. Grant to me the wisdom to help him/her
deal with that in the biblical patterns set forth in Your Word. In the
name of the Lord Jesus Christ and by the power of His blood, I
come against any spirit powers of darkness that are seeking to con-
trol and promote _____ patterns within _____'s life. I command any
spirit of _____ (name chief symptom) and all of his hosts to cease
this wicked work against _____, and you and your hosts must
leave _____ and go where the Lord Jesus Christ sends you.

Inability to Accept Limitations or Handicaps

If your child has a physical or mental disability, he may
feel bitterness or even despair at the limitations. One way you
can encourage and protect your child during his development
is to pray for him.

Dear heavenly Father, I thank You for _____ and even for the limi-
tations You have sovereignly allowed us to face in his/her life. I

*look to You to provide me Your wisdom, compassion, and care in
all the ways in which I relate to _____. In the name of the Lord
Jesus Christ and by the power of His blood, I come against any
powers of darkness that are seeking to create resentment, despair,
and bitterness within _____'s heart because of his/her limitations.
I renounce and resist all such efforts and I command them and all
of their hosts to leave _____'s presence, and they must go where the
Lord Jesus Christ sends them. I ask the Lord Jesus Christ to draw
_____ into such a personal, loving relationship with Himself that
_____ will be able to use (his/her) limitations in ways that will glorify God and encourage others.*

RESOURCES FOR PARENTS

Here are a variety of resources, including books and videotapes, to promote a child's security and thus help him or her
overcome the wolves of this world. The resources are in five
areas: (1) building a loving marriage, (2) communicating biblical sexual values, (3) modeling the responsible use of money,
(4) giving a balanced, biblical view of spiritual warfare issues,
and (5) understanding how to rear your children.

Building a Loving Marriage

Campbell, Ross. *How to Really Love Your Child*. Wheaton, Ill.:
Scripture Press, 1977.

Finzel, Hans, and Donna Finzel. *The Top Ten Ways to Drive Your
Wife Crazy—And How to Avoid Them*. Wheaton, Ill.: Victor,
1996.

Harley, Willard F., Jr. *His Needs, Her Needs*. Grand Rapids,
Mich.: Revell, 1994.

McDowell, Josh, and Dick Day. *How to Be a Hero to Your Kids*.
Dallas: Word, 1991.

Smith, Jim. *Learning to Live with the One You Love*. Carol
Stream, Ill.: Tyndale, 1991.

Trent, John. *Love for All Seasons: Eight Ways to Nurture Intimacy*. Chicago: Moody, 1996.

Wheat, Ed. *Love Life for Every Married Couple*. Grand Rapids,
Mich.: Zondervan, 1980.

Communicating Biblical Sexual Values

Learning About Sex Series. St. Louis, Mo.: Concordia, 1988.
This series is available in book and video form with helpful discussion sheets and leaders notes. The five books/videos, which are age-graded, are: *Why Boys & Girls Are Different* (ages 3 to 5), by Carol Greene; *Where Do Babies Come From?* (ages 6 to 8), by Ruth Hummel; *How You Are Changing* (ages 8 to 11), by Jane Graver; *Sex and the New You* (ages 11–14); and *Love, Sex & God* (ages 14 and up), by Bill Ameiss and Jane Graver.

God's Design for Sex Series. Colorado Springs: NavPress, 1994.
The four books in this series are: *The Story of Me*, by Stan and Brenna Jones; *Before I Was Born*, by Carolyn Nystrom; *What's the Big Deal*, by Stan and Brenna Jones; and *Facing the Facts*, by Stan and Brenna Jones.

Modeling the Responsible Use of Money

Briles, Judith. *Money Sense: What Every Woman Must Know to Be Financially Confident*. Chicago: Moody, 1994.
The Stewardship Series, by Larry Burkett. The first two books are very helpful in understanding the place of money and possessions in our lives: *Caretakers of God's Blessings: Using Our Resources Wisely* and *Where Your Treasure Is: Your Attitude on Finances* (Chicago: Moody, 1996).

      Larry Burkett has provided a wealth of materials that promote the biblical perspective of financial matters. These materials may be accessed by writing to: Christian Financial Concepts, P.O. Box 2377, Gainesville, GA 30503, or calling 1-800-722-1976.
Humber, Wilson J. *The Financially Challenged: Survival Guide for Getting Through the Week, the Month, and the Rest of Your Life*. Chicago: Moody, 1994.

Having a Balanced, Biblical View of Spiritual Warfare Issues

Anderson, Neil T. *Living Free in Christ*. Ventura, Calif.: Regal, 1993.
Bubeck, Mark I. *The Adversary*. Chicago: Moody, 1975.

Dickason, C. Fred. *Angels, Elect and Evil.* Chicago: Moody, 1975.

Logan, James. *Reclaiming Surrendered Ground.* Chicago: Moody, 1995.

Murphy, Ed. *Handbook for Spiritual Warfare.* Nashville: Nelson, 1992.

Warner, Timothy. *Spiritual Warfare.* Wheaton, Ill.: Crossway, 1991.

Wiersbe, Warren W. *The Strategy of Satan.* Wheaton, Ill.: Tyndale, 1985.

Rearing Our Children

Campbell, Ross. *Kids in Danger.* Wheaton, Ill.: Victor, 1995.

Dobson, James. *Parenting Isn't for Cowards.* Dallas: Word, 1987.

_____. *The New Dare to Discipline.* Wheaton, Ill.: Tyndale, 1992.

Johnson, Greg, and Mike Yorkey. *Faithful Parents, Faithful Kids.* Wheaton, Ill.: Tyndale, 1993.

Krueger, Caryl Waller. *365 Ways to Love Your Child.* Nashville: Abingdon, 1994.

Rogers, Adrian. *Ten Secrets for a Successful Family.* Wheaton, Ill.: Crossway, 1996.

Wright, H. Norman. *The Power Of a Parent's Words.* Ventura, Calif.: Regal, 1991.

SAYING "I LOVE YOU" TO OLDER CHILDREN

ometimes we think older children don't need to hear those words "I love you." *They are older, and they already know my love is there. They've seen it,* we tell ourselves. And it's true that sometimes our words of love to a teenager may bring an embarrassed silence or an "Oh, Mom!" especially if they're in public when we say it. But in truth, all kids love to know they're loved, even more so as they move through adolescence when self-doubt and a desire for acceptance increase.

There are many ways to express our love that go beyond the words. The following lists for junior and senior high school teens are only suggestive, not exhaustive. As I look back over these brief lists, I can see areas of need that deserve inclusion. Lift from my list what you recognize you need to use. Add things I've missed, but begin to communicate caring love at a meaningful level to your child. Nothing is of greater importance. For expressing your love to young children from ages one to twelve, look back under "How to Say 'I Love You'" in chapter 5.)

Saying "I Love You" to Junior High School Age Children

1. Honor individuality. If he enjoys hugs, OK, but don't offend if he thinks it's kids' stuff.

2. Listen to his quirks and concerns. If some new fad is unacceptable to you, take the time to explain why, offering well-thought-out reasons. Set fair, defined limits and expectations.

3. Reassure your child often that she is beautiful and special in both appearance and character qualities.

4. Plan meaningful and fun things that will include her happy participation with the whole family.

5. Set aside meaningful times for deeper talks about life choices and life decisions. Lunch or breakfast dates at a favorite restaurant open communication. Attending a family conference with your child, such as the Basic Life Principles seminar with Bill Gothard, may open good communication in these areas.

6. Include his closest friends in a planned outing of his choice. Accepting and influencing his friends for God and good are essential to good communication with a youth.

7. Build on the caring concern you've previously set by continuing to pray often in his hearing for the life partner of God's choice to be kept for him and he for her.

8. Keep the discipline needed in a form that honors your child's dignity and is not demeaning to her self-worth. Most junior high young people are beyond the age where physical spankings will be beneficial.

9. Commend your child often for character development, significant accomplishments, and spiritual virtues.

10. Watch for ways to help your child know that you think your marriage partner—his dad or mom—is the dearest person in the world to you. Knowing your love for the

other parent makes him sense your love for him.

Saying "I Love You" to High School Age Children

1. Have regular times conducive to talking about important topics. Breakfast dates or lunch dates between an individual parent and his high schooler can be as important as what might be said.

2. Express apologies when appropriate concerning wrong decisions or actions you've made concerning your high schooler. Even confess wrong attitudes if they exist.

3. Convey your desire to honor him or her more and more as an adult who can come to you as a counselor and guidance resource. Let her know that at this stage you still retain veto power on issues you consider very important.

4. Hug and verbalize often your love for your teen.

5. Watch for little ways to communicate caring love by notes, words, gifts, and commendations.

6. Provide a list of colleges, Bible institutes, or universities that you find acceptable. Ask your high schooler to begin to pray and study each school to determine which one might be God's appointed place for higher education.

7. Pray more seriously for God to keep your teen for another, and vice versa, in His sovereign plan for a life partner.

8. Talk about life work choices as well as gifts and interests you've noted that please you.

9. Keep eye contact at all times during your conversations.

10. Let your teen hear you pray about stressful times, tests, personal relationships, and any concerns that teens carry.

A MODEL PRAYER FOR PROTECTING CHILDREN FROM SPIRITISTIC HARASSMENT

The following prayer can help parents who sense any powers of darkness may be harassing their children. I recommend proper preparation, including fasting and personal prayer (see p. 179), before a parent uses this prayer on behalf of the child. Jesus warned us that replacement demonic powers can invade a person once other powers are removed (Matthew 12:43–45); therefore this prayer contains a call to "bind all [the] hosts who work with" any demonic influences, including "replacer powers of darkness," and bans the "restructuring, regrouping, or multiplying of the activity of the powers of darkness."

🕊 🕊 🕊 🕊

Loving heavenly Father, (I/we) welcome your protective presence with us in this time of prayer. I ask You to assign Your holy angels to protect and guard us and our children with their guarding protection during this time of prayer.

In the mighty name of our Lord Jesus Christ and by the power of His blood I command all powers of darkness not having assignment against us or our family to leave our presence. They may not intrude or in any way seek to disrupt this confrontation against powers of darkness seeking to afflict and control _____. I also ask that all powers of darkness that Satan has assigned to rule over _____ be subdued and forbidden to work in any way against _____ while (he/she) sleeps.

Thank You, Lord Jesus Christ, that You promised to never leave us or forsake us. I welcome Your unseen presence here in this room with us. It's in Your mighty name, Lord Jesus Christ, that I take authority over those forces of darkness seeking to harass and rule over my child. As the spiritual and parental guardian of _____ and as one who is seated with You in the heavenly realms, I use my authority in Christ to command all powers of darkness seeking to control _____ to be bound here in the presence of the Lord Jesus Christ.

(At this point refer to your prepared list of suspected activities of powers of darkness. Use the name of the symptom you see to identify the suspected strongholds. They and your Lord know their identity. Proceed with this kind of prayer.)

I pull in and bind before the Lord Jesus Christ all powers of darkness working against _____ in footholds and strongholds of _____ (name those workings of darkness you believe are troubling your child, such as fear, hate, lust, rage, etc.). I command that they become and remain whole spirits. I bind all their hosts who work with them, all backup systems and replacer powers of darkness. There may be no restructuring, regrouping, or multiplying of the activity of the powers of darkness assigned against _____. In the name of my Lord Jesus Christ and by the power of His blood, I command these powers of darkness to give full attention to what my Lord Jesus Christ will say to you.

I now ask You, Lord Jesus Christ, in that spiritual realm where You dwell with me, and where these powers of darkness know Your presence, to tell these scheming, troubling forces of evil where they must go. I want them to leave ____ and our family totally and completely. I ask You to insure that they go where they cannot return to continue their evil work. (A pause of reverent waiting for our Lord to address His will and authority over them is in order.)

I now ask that the Holy Spirit would evict from ____'s presence all these powers of darkness. They must go where the Lord Jesus Christ has commanded them to go. I ask the Spirit to make a thorough search in and around ____ to make sure that there are no lingering forces of evil to deceive and rule over ____. May the Holy Spirit sanctify ____'s whole person from the defiling works of darkness. I invite the Lord Jesus Christ by the power of the Holy Spirit to do Your great work of drawing ____ to Yourself for blessings and spiritual growth.

Thank You, loving heavenly Father, for the faith and grace You have given to me to use my authority in Christ to stand in watchful protection over ____. I yield fully to Your plan and purpose for this battle. Grant to me the wisdom and grace to protect my family, and guide each one into Your plan and will. I worship You and give You thanks in the name of my Lord Jesus Christ. Amen.

QUESTIONNAIRE FOR THOSE DESIRING SPIRITUAL GROWTH

The first step in the seven steps to freedom outlined in chapter 10 is to renounce all involvements with false religions, occult practices, divinations, magic, sorcery, witchcraft, spiritistic healings, séances, and similar activities. The following questionnaire can help you recall those involvements past or present that can be giving the Enemy a foothold in your life. (This is an abridged form of a fuller questionnaire that also explores past emotional and physical traumas as well as emotional problems and conflicts.)

As you complete the questionnaire, consider both past and present involvements. Check all blanks that apply.

1. Occult Activity

_____ Have you ever visited a fortune teller who told your fortune by :

cards_____ tea leaves_____ palm reading _____

other (please specify)_____ ?

_____ Do you read or follow the horoscope?

_____ Have you ever played with games of an occult nature, such as

ESP_____ Kabul_____

other (specify)_____ ?

_____ Have you ever consulted out of curiosity or interest:

Ouija® board_____ planchette_____

crystal ball_____ tea leaves_____

other (specify) _____ ?

_____ Have you ever had a "life" or reincarnation reading?

_____ Have you

had your handwriting analyzed_____

practiced mental suggestion_____

cast a magic spell_____

or sought psychic experience_____ ?

_____ Have you practiced mystical meditation?

_____ Do you now, or have you ever, had a "spirit guide"?

_____ Have you ever seen or been involved in Satan worship?

_____ Are you now, or have you ever been, a practicing witch?

_____ Have you ever had an imaginary playmate?

_____ Have you practiced any of the martial arts (karate, etc.)?

_____ Have you practiced mind control as in Sylon, Pathways, Zen Buddhism, etc.?

2. Cults with Which Connected
(*Directly or Indirectly*)

_____ Hare Krishna

_____ Unitarian

_____ Scientology

_____ Jehovah's Witnesses

_____ Zen Buddhism

_____ Unification Church (Moon)

_____ Meher Baba

_____ Theosophy

_____ Hippie-ism

_____ Inner Peace Movement

_____ Rosicrucianism

_____ Gurdjieff Foundation

_____ Religious Research of America (The Fourth Way)

_____ The Way International

_____ Metropolitan Community (MCC: homosexual emphasis)

_____ The Local Church

_____ Other (specify): _____

_____ Spiritual Frontier Fellowship

_____ Church of Jesus Christ (cult name)

_____ Children of God

_____ LDS (Mormons)

_____ Christian Science

_____ Transcendental Meditation

_____ Baha'i World Faith

_____ est

_____ Unity

Ritual Practices, Readings, or Use of Objects

_____ Have you ever sought, or been subject to as a child, healing through magic conjurations and charming, such as the removal of warts and burns, treatment of disease, etc., through

a spiritualist_____

Christian Science healer_____

spirit healer_____

psychic healer_____

metaphysical use of pendulum_____

hypnosis _____

trance for diagnosis_____?

other occult means (specify):

_____

Have you ever been given or worn an amulet, talisman, or charm for luck or protection?

_____ Have you ever sought to locate missing persons or objects by consulting someone with psychic, clairvoyant, or psychometric powers?

_____ Have you ever participated in "I Ching"?

_____ Have you, or has anyone for you, practiced water witching (sometimes called dowsing or divining) to locate water, etc., using a twig or pendulum?

_____ Do you read or possess occult or spiritualist literature such as books on

astrology_____   fortune telling_____

interpretation of   black magic_____
dreams_____
                                       ESP_____
religious cults_____
                                       clairvoyance_____
self-realization_____
                                       psychic phenomena_____?

occult magical books such as *Secrets of Psalms* or the so-called *Sixth* and *Seventh Books of Moses*_____?

_____ Have you ever experimented or practiced

extrasensory perception _____

telepathy _____?

_____ Have you practiced any form of magic charming or ritual?

_____ Do you possess any occult or pagan religious objects, relics, or artifacts which may have been used in pagan temples and religious rites, or in the practice of sorcery, magic, divination, or spiritualism?

Consciousness Problems

_____ Lost awareness of time (from minutes to hours), ending up someplace and not knowing how you got there

_____ Extreme sleepiness during discussion of spiritual things

_____ Demonstration of extraordinary abilities (either ESP or telekinesis)

_____ Hearing of voices in the mind (they mock, intimidate, accuse, threaten, or bargain)

_____ Voice speaking from the subject (yourself or a relative) that refers to (him/her) in the third person

_____ Supernatural experiences, such as haunting, the movement or disappearance of objects

A MODEL PRAYER FOR CONTINUING RESISTANCE TO DEMONIC INFLUENCE

This wrap-up prayer is wise to use after going through the steps to freedom. It can help those dealing with generational transfer and other issues of demonic influence to effectively resist the Devil. During counseling, I sometimes ask the counselee to repeat the prayer after me. I pause and give the person the opportunity to repeat the words. The advantage of doing it that way is the support it gives. Whether you have a close friend lead you in the prayer, or do it privately, understand that neither these words nor my background is responsible for the freeing that results. You are using the believer's own authority to claim their freedom in Christ. As indicated at the end of chapter 10, you are welcome to copy this prayer and keep it convenient for use.

🕿 🕿 🕿 🕿

I worship and honor my heavenly Father, the Lord Jesus Christ, and the Holy Spirit; the true and living God who promised, "I will never leave you or forsake you." I welcome and honor the unseen presence of my Lord Jesus Christ who promised always to be with us when we meet in His name. I honor and thank You, Lord Jesus Christ, for Your invisible presence in this very place with us. I ask You to be in charge and to effect only Your will and plan in our lives. I yield fully to Your will in the eviction of any and all wicked spirit control from my life. I desire the Holy Spirit to do the sanctifying work within my whole person and being that He is there to accomplish. I ask You, Lord Jesus Christ, to assign Your holy angels to protect us from any strategies of darkness designed to oppose this prayer for freedom. Keep Satan and all his opposing hosts of evil away from us. I also ask You to insure that wicked spirits evicted from my presence will depart quickly and directly to the place to which You consign them.

In the name of my Lord Jesus Christ and by the power of His blood, I affirm my authority over all wicked spirits assigned to control me and hinder my life and my witness for Christ. I now command all lingering wicked spirits assigned to harass, rule, and control me to cease their work and be bound in the presence of the Lord Jesus Christ. I bind all backup systems and replacer wicked spirits assigned to rebuild evicted strongholds. They may not do that! I command all those spirits assigned against me to be and remain whole spirits. I forbid any dividing, restructuring, or multiplying of wicked spirit workings against me. There is to be one-way traffic of evil spirit activity out of my life and to the place that the Lord Jesus Christ consigns them. I pull in from other family members all those wicked spirits working under the chain of authority established by the powers of darkness assigned to rule over me. I command them all to be bound together here in the presence of my Lord Jesus Christ in that spiritual realm where He dwells with me and they know His presence. It is my will that all powers of darkness having assignment against me must hear and obey Him who is their Creator and Conqueror. I command their full attention to the Lord Jesus Christ. I declare Him to be my Redeemer and Lord. I affirm that God has seated me with Christ Jesus in the heavenly realms far above all principalities and supernatural powers of darkness and evil.

Lord Jesus Christ, I ask You to tell all of these powers of darkness assigned to afflict and rule over me where they must go. I want them out of my life and confined where they can never trouble me again. I yield fully to Your sovereign plan for my life and all of the purposes You have in this battle I have been facing. I ask You, Lord Jesus Christ, to tell them clearly where they must go.

(A brief pause is in order to honor the Lord Jesus Christ's work of addressing His authority and victory against those powers of darkness bound in accountability before Him.)

I now ask the Holy Spirit dwelling within my person to effect the will of the Lord Jesus Christ concerning these afflicting powers of darkness. Just as You forced them out of people's lives in response to Jesus' commands when He walked on this earth, I ask You to accomplish that for me now. I ask You, Spirit of the living God, to evict from my conscious, subconscious, and unconscious mind all control of any wicked powers. Break all of their power and manipulation of my thought processes. They must go where the Lord Jesus Christ sends them. Sweep them away and make my mind clear of any wicked spirit dominion. I now ask that the Holy Spirit would renew and sanctify my mind. Cleanse and take full possession of my conscious, unconscious, and subconscious mind, precious Holy Spirit. Set it totally apart for the glory of God and the service of my Lord Jesus Christ. I deliberately yield my mind to the lordship of Christ, the truth of God's Word, and the will of my heavenly Father.

I now ask that the Holy Spirit would look all through my emotions on the conscious, subconscious, and unconscious level. Evict any controlling powers of darkness and may the holy angels escort them to the place where the Lord Jesus Christ is commanding them to go. Clean them out and take them totally away from my person. I ask that the gracious Holy

Spirit would take control of my emotions on every level of the function of my feelings. Sanctify my emotions. Fill my emotions with the Spirit's fruit of love, joy, peace, patience, gentleness, meekness, faithfulness, and self-control. I welcome the Holy Spirit's internal control of my feelings. I look to the Spirit of God to sanctify and renew my emotions. I reach out to experience the Lord's plan for my emotional freedom and spiritual well-being.

I now ask that the Holy Spirit would look all through my conscious, unconscious, and subconscious will for any control of wicked powers. Evict them now to where the Lord Jesus Christ is commanding them to go. Sweep my volition totally clean from evil control and manipulation. May the Holy Spirit of the true and living God renew and sanctify my will fully for the glory of God. Will within me to do God's good will. May the lordship of Jesus Christ be obediently lived out in my life by the Holy Spirit's enabling control of my will.

I offer my body in all of its parts and functions as an expression of my spiritual worship to my heavenly Father. I ask the Holy Spirit to look all through my body for any controlling activity of wicked spirits. Look all through my brain and central nervous system for any fallen spirit's affliction or control. Evict them totally away from this physical control center for the function of my mind and body. I offer my brain and its capacities for the quickening, renewing control of the Holy Spirit. Sanctify and refresh my brain so that it functions in spiritual harmony with Your control of my whole person. Look all through my body and sever any wicked spirit control of my senses of vision, hearing, smell, touch, or taste. Look all through the organs of my body for any defiling work of the kingdom of darkness. Sanctify my body's organs and their function by the quickening work of the Holy Spirit.

I surrender all my physical appetites to Your lordship. I give to You my need and craving for food and drink. Examine and cleanse from demonic activity all the organs of my digestive system. Set apart my sexuality for the glory of God. Evict any work of the Enemy in my sexual functions and organs. I surrender these to Your lordship, and I submit myself to Your holy plan for moral purity and sexual intimacy only in the bonds of marriage.

Evict any afflicting, evil powers totally away from every part of my body. Sanctify it in its entirety. I want my body to be a "holy body," not only in its standing in God's redemptive plan but also in its function. As a part of my spiritual worship to my Father in heaven, I offer my body as a living sacrifice to be used only for all that is acceptable in His sight.

I now yield up my whole person again to the true and living God and His full control. I ask the Father, Son, and Holy Spirit to control me fully. I thank You for the freedom that You have effected within me during this time of prayer. I now look to the love of my heavenly Father, the lordship of Jesus Christ, and the ministry of the Holy Spirit to enable me to daily walk in the spiritual freedom promised me in God's holy Word. I reject, resist, and refuse anything less. In the name and worthiness of my Lord Jesus Christ and by the intercessions of the Holy Spirit, I place these petitions before my Father in heaven.

NOTES

Chapter 3: The Delayed-Harvest Principle

1. Timothy M. Warner, *Spiritual Warfare* (Wheaton, Ill.: Crossway, 1991), 107.
2. Here are four: Neil T. Anderson, *The Bondage Breaker* (Eugene, Oreg.: Harvest, 1990); C. Fred Dickason, *Demon Possession and the Christian* (Westchester, Ill.: Crossway, 1989); Jim Logan, *Reclaiming Surrendered Ground* (Chicago: Moody, 1995); and Ed Murphy, *The Handbook for Spiritual Warfare* (Nashville, Tenn.: Nelson, 1992).
3. D. M. Lloyd-Jones, *Romans—An Exposition of Chapter 5* (Grand Rapids, Mich.: Zondervan, 1971), 196.
4. G. Campbell Morgan, *The Westminster Pulpit*, vol. 4 (London: Pickering & Inglis, n.d.), 50.
5. John MacArthur, Jr., *How to Meet the Enemy* (Wheaton, Ill.:, Victor, 1992), 136.
6. Gerhard Kittel and Gerhard Friedrich, *Theological Dictionary of the New Testament*, vol. 5, (Grand Rapids, Mich.: Eerdmans, 1968), 638.
7. G. Campbell Morgan, *The Great Physician* (New York: Revell, n.d.), 189–90.
8. Murphy, *The Handbook For Spiritual Warfare*, 437–38.
9. C. Fred Dickason, *Demon Possession and the Christian*, 221.
10. Mark I. Bubeck, *Overcoming the Adversary* (Chicago: Moody, 1984), 29–30.
11. Be aware that satanic ritual abuse more often is passed to your children by the culture. Organized satanic cults are growing in popularity among those rebellious against God. Little children, especially children of Christian believers, are often targeted by these cultists for exposure to SRA. Accessing children of believers is thought to bring them more favor and power from Satan's kingdom.

    Although we do not want to promote fear, a warning is in order. Be very guarded about allowing your children to participate in "slumber parties" ("sleepovers") with school friends or neighborhood families you do not know. Similarly, be careful in selecting baby-sitters and child-care providers; cultists often seek to provide such care for access to children for cult rituals.

Chapter 4: Parents Who Love Each Other

1. See Matthew 5:13–16; Mark 4:21–23; and Luke 8:16–18.
2. The book, first published in 1977, is still in print. A companion volume, *How*

to Love Your Teenager, first published in 1981, also remains in print (Dutton, 1994).

3. Ross Campbell, *How to Really Love Your Child* (Wheaton, Ill.: Victor, 1977), 22, 32.

4. Josh McDowell and Dick Day, *How to Be a Hero to Your Kids* (Dallas: Word, 1991), 9.

5. Ibid., 10–11.

6. Ibid., 11.

7. In "Resources for Parents," page 223, I recommend seven books on strengthening your marriage in the section "Building a Loving Marriage."

8. If you need help in developing "clear the air" times, consider a weekend Marriage Encounter retreat (call 800-795-LOVE). Or attend a marriage retreat with your own denominational group that includes times of one-on-one dialogue with your spouse.

9. The Lord Jesus Christ understood this basic need of children. He took them in His arms and put His hands on them. That's the way He blessed them. He touched them! See Mark 10:13–14, 16.

Chapter 5: Parents Who Communicate

1. In fact, my surprised mother said, "Mark, you did that last year." I'm sure I did; but my new birth happened one year later, when I was eight. My prior "doing that" may have been because others were making decisions and I thought I should make one too. Peer pressure got a response that was not genuine. God's work of saving grace was real at age eight, when I truly invited Christ into my life. Parents should never criticize a child for making a salvation decision a second time; it may be a genuine conversion.

2. Mark Bubeck, *The Adversary* (Chicago: Moody, 1975), 117–22.

3. Two resources that can facilitate communication with your children on the music issue are: Frank Garlock, *Music in the Balance* (Greenville, S.C.: Majesty Music, 1993). (Garlock also has six videotapes discussing music theory and its application to biblical principles. Write him at Majesty Music Co., P.O. Box 654, Greenville, SC,; and Al Menconi and Dave Hart, *Today's Music: A Window to Your Child's Soul* (Colorado Springs: Cook, 1990).

Chapter 6: Freeing Our Children

1. Here is a model prayer you can use to renounce any transfer claims from close relatives: "In the name of my Lord Jesus Christ and by the power of His blood, I forbid any demonic activity to transfer to me or my family because of the ground being given by (name of close relative). I ask my Lord Jesus Christ to set a holy watch of the holy angels about us all to insure that no such transfer may be possible. I commit our whole family to the sealing, protective care of the Holy Spirit."

2. The belief that people have two parts is called the "dichotomist view" and traces back to the Greek philosopher Plato. Plato gave the soul a much higher place of importance. He thought the soul existed in "the heavenly world of pure form or idea before its incarnation in the human body" (Wayne E. Ward in Everett F. Harrison, ed., *Baker's Dictionary of Theology* [Grand Rapids, Mich.: Baker, 1960], 166). The philosopher Aristotle seems to have initiated the "Trichotomist view" that the soul actually has a twofold division: the animal soul (organic aspects) and the rational soul (intellectual aspects).

Though doubtless influenced by the Greek philosophers, theologians and early Christian writers derive their insights more from their study and understanding of the Bible. Trichotomists, such as Origen, found texts like Hebrews 4:12 and 1 Thessalonians 5:23 supportive, if not conclusive evidence, of the tripartite nature of man's being. Tertullian and Augustine are among other early Christian writers who support the dichotomist view. They look at terms such as *soul*, *heart*, and *spirit* in Scripture and see them all as describing aspects and functions of the soul.

Although conservative theologians from both perspectives may differ sharply over some elements, the differences are usually charitably held and seldom result in a disrupted fellowship. Both views recognize the importance of the fundamental wholeness and unity of the human person.

3. For an in-depth presentation of how the Devil uses various outside arenas to threaten our spirit and soul, consult the video presentation "Interfacing Our Three Enemies," from the International Center for Biblical Counseling (ICBC), 1551 Indian Hills Dr., Suite 200, Sioux City, IA 51104. The ICBC also has several audiotape series on Satan's influence on our lives; write ICBC for a complete catalogue.

4. In a previous book, the author has prepared a biblical study of Satan and his kingdom in careful detail. In the interests of brevity, and to avoid redundancy, the reader is urged to use that study to better understand the organized structure and activity of the kingdom of darkness. This outline is not meant to be a full biblical definition. See: Mark I. Bubeck, *The Adversary* (Chicago: Moody, 1975), 55.

5. For a greater understanding of the often misunderstood filling of the Holy Spirit, read Lewis Sperry Chafer, *Systematic Theology*, vol. 1, abridged ed. (Grand Rapids, Mich.: Kregel, 1993), 260–77.

Chapter 7: Freedom for Parents

1. The reader will do well to learn the various views of depravity. I recommend the discussions of this concept in Lewis Sperry Chafer, *Systematic Theology*, 8 vols. in 4, vol. 1 (Grand Rapids, Mich.: Kregel, 1993), 376–86; Charles C. Ryrie, *Basic Theology* (Wheaton, Ill.: Victor, 1986), 201–21.

Chapter 9: Spiritistic Activity in Children

1. For an in-depth look at the ministries of angels, both good and evil, see C. Fred Dickason, *Angels, Elect And Evil* (Chicago: Moody, 1975).

2. Neil T. Anderson and Steve Russo, *The Seduction of Our Children* (Eugene, Oreg.: Harvest House, 1991).

3. Two books that are very helpful in understanding occult and satanic symbols and other clues to a child's interest in supernatural evil are: Johanna Michaelsen, *Like Lambs to the Slaughter* (Eugene, Ore.: Harvest, 1989); and Anderson and Russo, *The Seduction of Our Children*.

Chapter 10: Applying the Steps to Freedom

1. Neil T. Anderson, *The Bondage Breaker* (Eugene, Oreg. Harvest, 1990), 185–212.

2. Here is a model prayer you can use to renounce past sexual immorality: "I confess and renounce my sinful sexual union with (name of person or persons) as a sin against God and my own body. I ask the cleansing blood of my Lord Jesus Christ to free me from the guilt and ground I've given by my sex-

ual union with _____. I renounce all bonding oneness with _____ that took place in the sexual act, and I ask that I be freed from the consequences of that bonding. I renounce all wicked spirits that have transferred claim against me because of that sexual sin. In the name of my Lord Jesus Christ, I break and renounce all transfer claim. I ask the Lord Jesus Christ to send any and all transferred powers of darkness to where He wants them to go."

3. In addition to occult practices, alcoholism, and gambling addictions, here are other practices or behavior traits that have considerable significance and you may look for: clairvoyance, magic, mystical healings, ability to "witch" a well, extrasensory perception, secret lodge oaths and participation, addiction to harmful music, anger, immoral conduct, stealing, lying, violence, drug addiction, lawlessness, false religious practices, rebellion, arrogant pride, hate, bitterness, suicide, jealousy, quarreling, abusive behavior, sexual perversion, cruelty, and vile language.

Emotional responses and practices that deserve consideration are: fear, shyness, loneliness, withdrawal, laziness, aloofness, brashness, crudity, manipulation, pouting, accusing, faultfinding, gossip, backbiting, paranoia, deep depression, aloneness, greed, and inability to show love.

Chapter 11: Prayer That Defeats the Rule of Evil

1. In addition, single parents have special concerns for their children that often create fears. Here is a prayer for single parents feeling burdened in protecting their children from demonic influences:

"Heavenly Father, I bring the burden of being a single parent to You for Your wisdom, strength, and sustaining courage. I resist all efforts of darkness to put upon me attitudes of resentment and self-pity that would only further harm the children and me. I ask You to guide and encourage me through Your Word. I reach out to You and look to You for Your provision in all of my personal and family needs. I hold that victorious name of my Lord Jesus Christ over my children and me that we may walk in His provided victory for each day. May Your guarding, protecting angels be assigned to minister to us in our needs as You determine best. Help me to be loving and submissive to You in everything. Help me to trust You with my future in every detail of life."